Before Becoming This

Shree Maa

Swami Satyananda Saraswati

BEFORE
BECOMING THIS

Conversations with
Shree Maa and Swami Satyananda
About Life, Love and the Cosmic Play

by

Steven Newmark, Ph.D.

Devi Mandir Publications

CONTENTS

Relationships With Divinity

Planet Earth

BOOK THREE · CONVERSATIONS WITH SHREE MAA AND SWAMI SATYANANDA

Relationships

The Human Melodrama

BOOK FOUR · PUTTING IT ALL INTO PRACTICE

OPENING

I first met Shree Maa and Swami Satyananda on a crisp, fall day in 1995. I had been trying to wrangle an invitation to see Shree Maa since reading about her in Linda Johnsen's book, *Daughters of the Goddess: The Women Saints of India*. Linda had described Shree Maa as an enlightened being, and I was surprised that a person of her stature was living in Napa, an hour from my Bay area home.

I had visited people who were said to be enlightened before, including Anandamaya Ma, Amachi, Mother Meera and several great Tibetan Rimpoches. I had even spent several weeks in India with the advaita master, Shri Poonja. Meeting these beings was usually an inspiring experience, so I was excited by the prospect of finding a saint in my own backyard. I was also a little nervous.

After walking up a long hill (you have to pay something to see a Guru), I heard chanting coming from a rustic looking, glass and wood frame building. Once inside, I noticed a roaring fire spewing billowing smoke, surrounded by about forty people chanting intently.

I looked around for Shree Maa, but I didn't see anyone who looked like a Guru. What drew my attention was the man leading the chanting. He was about fifty, bearded and wearing the orange robes of a Swami. To my surprise, he was a Westerner. He was chanting with such passion and abandon that I was immediately drawn to him. Here was a man enjoying himself and not playing the pious role of the sanctimonious spiritual teacher. "Thank God," I thought, "at least this is going to be fun."

After a few minutes, I noticed a small Indian woman sitting about ten feet away from the Swami. I wondered if this was Shree Maa. She was so small and slight that she seemed almost invisible. Instead of sitting on an elevated platform with a special seat separate from others, she was sitting on the floor with everyone else. I doubted that this could be the saint I was looking for.

When the ceremony was over, I was disappointed to find that this woman was indeed Shree Maa. I had hoped to meet a powerful Guru who would knock me off my feet with her presence and charisma. My reflections were interrupted by the friend who had invited me to this event. He asked if I'd like to meet Shree Maa. I agreed, surprised by this unexpected opportunity.

He took me to the front of the temple grounds. It was a simple tableau: some trees, a few benches and a dirt road that curved around the temple building. Shree Maa stood twenty feet in front of us. At the moment I saw her, an Indian man had fallen to his knees in pranam, the traditional Indian greeting to a Guru. He touched his head all the way to the ground with deep respect. When it was my turn to greet Shree Maa, I followed the Indian man's lead and also got down on my knees and put my head to the ground in pranam. This was a new experience for me, and although I felt awkward and self-conscious, there was something intrinsically pleasing about that act of surrender. Later I discovered that most people greet Shree Maa in the more traditionally Western, vertical fashion.

When I rose to my feet, an odd event occurred. Although I stand six feet three inches, and Shree Maa is five feet five inches, she appeared taller than me, and I had the sensation of looking up into her eyes. What I saw at that moment shocked me. Her eyes looked like the clear, unclouded sky. I saw no pupils or irises — just blank, white eyes. They looked translucent and emitted a powerful, electric energy. I was awestruck. It didn't seem like there was anybody inside her body. She appeared completely empty of a separate personality.

A few minutes after this experience, I thought of an old friend who, when meeting Anandamaya Ma in India, said that he saw the ocean when he looked into her eyes. I always imagined he meant an ocean with waves, but now I thought he might have seen the calm, blue, infinite ocean, which was what I saw reflected in Shree Maa's eyes. After that meeting, I drove home in a daze. I felt I had just encountered something from a different world.

As Westerners, we have little preparation for this kind of experience. A survey conducted by *Newsweek* magazine indicated that a majority of Americans have experienced events that were discontinuous from their normal reality, experiences they might call miracles. However, because they have no context for understanding these events, they are often dismissed as aberrations or hallucinations. Easterners, operating from a different cultural paradigm, also experience these same sorts of events but honor them as sacred blessings.

In the West, we are even less prepared for the concept or experience of an enlightened being. We have witnessed an influx of "holy men" from the East who ended up sleeping with their disciples or acquiring fifty Rolls Royces. The term "Guru" has become so devalued in the West that we even hear football coaches and car mechanics referred to in this way.

Fortunately, I had studied the philosophy of the East and had visited India. I was somewhat familiar with the context in which a person like Shree Maa could be understood. After that first meeting, I was drawn to see her again, even though I wondered if what I had experienced wasn't just my imagination. If it was at all possible, I wanted to get to know this Shree Maa and find out who she really was.

Later, I did get the opportunity to spend time with Shree Maa and I learned parts of her life story in bits and pieces. I discovered that from birth, Shree Maa did not cry. It was even difficult to determine when she was hungry or needed to be changed. Miracles reportedly abounded during her childhood, including the phenomenon that whenever she wanted something, it appeared.

Evidently, Shree Maa was a happy and popular child, but she was constantly drawn to leave home and spend all her time absorbed in God. At the age of seven, she wandered into the forest to meet with sadhus, people who have renounced their material attachments in pursuit of a spiritual life. Even though she felt a strong desire to join these sadhus who freely shared their wisdom with her, Shree Maa knew that her work in this lifetime required her to finish school and earn a Bachelor of Arts degree.

After graduating from college, Shree Maa left home to wander in the jungles of India, oblivious to any impending danger. "What risk, what fear?" she later joked with disciples. "When I am one with the soul of existence, how will anyone or anything cause me harm?" She carried only the simple cloth she was wearing and went for days without food. She would sit by a river or at the foot of a tree and experience samadhi (deep absorption in God) for long periods. Sometimes, when she opened her eyes, she would find many village people sitting before her in silent respect. Then she would sing about her love for God with a pure, melodious voice.

Over one period of eight years, Shree Maa's daily meal consisted of a little piece of turmeric and basil leaves washed down with some sandal paste mixed with water. Her weight dropped to sixty pounds. It was during this time that she allowed disciples to gather around her, and Shree Maa became a well-known saint in the northeastern part of India.

In 1980, she met Swami Satyananda, a Westerner who had decided as a young man to travel around the world before settling down as a corporate lawyer. However, the passion and wisdom of India were so compelling that he just couldn't leave. At the time he met Shree Maa, he had already lived in India for fifteen years and had been ordained as a full Swami. He even had disciples of his own. Five years later, Shree Maa and Swami Satyananda came to the United States to bring the teachings of the East to the West. I will tell you more about Swami Satyananda in the second section of this book.

As I got to know Shree Maa better, I continued to be surprised by her humility and egolessness. Deepak Chopra called her the "elegance of simplicity," and Linda Johnsen said about her, "Shree Maa is completely transparent, almost invisible. There is no agitation in her whatsoever; it is as if the air itself is not disturbed when she passes by." Her humility said to me, "I am no different from you. We are all divine beings." In fact, I discovered that this is one of her central teachings. To Shree Maa everyone is God, and she is just living the "natural life of a human being," someone who experiences the truth of who we all really are.

I was also impressed with the depth of Shree Maa's wisdom. Whatever suggestions she made to me had an immediate, positive impact on my life. It was as if she understood aspects of me that I wasn't yet in touch with. When she spoke, it sounded and felt like "the truth."

For me Shree Maa's most attractive quality was her obvious, unbounded joy. She seemed extremely happy almost all the time. It's the kind of happiness that is so deep and intrinsic that nothing seems to shake it. She often acted like a carefree, young girl, bubbling over with exuberance and love. While in her presence, I got a "contact high," and my consciousness was automatically elevated.

I had considered myself a relatively happy person when I first met Shree Maa. I had a good relationship, satisfying work, close friends and a nice home in Marin County. But something fundamental was missing. When I started spending time with Shree Maa and Swami and, in particular, began to meditate in the way they taught me, I felt a significant and immediate shift. I began experiencing a profound sense of peace and happiness. While going about routine, daily tasks, the thought "I love my life!" would spontaneously come to my mind. At this point in my life, I would say this happiness has matured into true joy.

The more time I spent with Shree Maa and Swami Satyananda, the more questions I accumulated: What is it like to be enlightened? How does one become enlightened? Do I even want to become enlightened? (After all, what will happen to "me" if "I" am not around any more?) What is the purpose of relationships? What happens after death? And on and on. My desire to have these questions answered coalesced into the creation of this book.

The first section of *Before Becoming This* is a series of candid interviews with Shree Maa. In the second section, Swami Satyananda tells his story of traveling through India and explains the context for understanding enlightenment and Indian spirituality. In the third section, Shree Maa and Swami together discuss relationships, Ramakrishna and the cosmic play. In the final section, Swami Satyananda offers practical suggestions for how to put all this information into use so that it can directly impact our lives.

· BOOK ONE ·
CONVERSATIONS WITH
SHREE MAA

"TRUE SPIRITUALITY IS WHEN YOU GIVE MORE THAN YOU TAKE."

— Shree Maa

Introduction To Shree Maa

These interviews that follow are the first of this kind that Shree Maa has ever given. In fact, Swami Satyananda, the person who knows her the best, didn't even think she would allow herself to be interviewed. Until now, Shree Maa has shunned publicity and is so unassuming she hasn't even read the biography that Swami Satyananda wrote about her.

In the first interview, Shree Maa tells us her life story. The subsequent interviews, which cover a wide variety of topics, are unusual, because in them Shree Maa shares with us the experiences and world view of an enlightened being.

All these interviews were filled with incredible joy and sweetness. Shree Maa punctuated most statements with a smile, a laugh or a giggle. Her love and cosmic sense of humor underscored everything she talked about. Her nonverbal communication said, "Don't worry, God is taking care of everything."

1
MY LIFE IN INDIA

A Soul Is Coming

Before I was born my parents lived in Assam, India, a mountainous region a short distance from Tibet, Burma and China. My mom was very young when she married and was only fourteen years old when she became pregnant with me.

One day, two months after the beginning of my mom's pregnancy, my parents went on a pilgrimage to the Kamakhya Temple, which was the most famous temple in the area. At that time you had to travel by foot, so if you left in the morning, you wouldn't get to the temple until evening. When they finally reached the temple and walked up a long flight of steps to the top, a highly respected Guru was standing and watching them intently. He approached my parents and said, "I have been waiting for you for a long time. Please come with me. I would like to give both of you initiation. A soul is coming to you who will do lots of work for this universe." My parents were very surprised.

The Guru's name was Bhuvananda Saraswati. He initiated my parents and told them to come back for another initiation two months after their daughter was born.

When I was two months old, they visited the Guru again, and he was so happy to see me! He held me in his arms and danced around the room. Then he gave me an initiation by speaking a mantra into my ear. He also gave my mom and dad another initiation. When he initiated my mom, she levitated. She hovered three feet above the ground. Her third eye was glowing like a ping-pong ball. The experience was so powerful that even the Guru became a little afraid. My mom was so pure that the Guru and she were like a match and paper. When they were put together, they ignited. The Guru meditated and recited mantras, and slowly my mom came back to the ground and regained normal consciousness.

Grandma

My mom told me that when I was a little child I never cried. It was hard for her to know when to feed me milk. About one year after I was born, my mom became pregnant again. Because she was too young to raise two infants, my grandma ended up taking care of me. She was my real mother.

My grandma was an efficient, strict and disciplined woman. She was also very spiritual. She prayed in the morning,

afternoon and evening. She was a devotee of Ramakrishna (a 19th-century Indian saint) and sang his songs at night and told me lots of spiritual stories. She molded me with God.

I can remember one of the stories my grandma told me. This story was about a naked saint who was three hundred years old. His name was Trailinga Swami. In the story some children were playing a game where they were pretending to cook with stones. They said, "This rock is the rice, this rock is the dahl and this one is the vegetable." The saint came up to them and said, "I am very hungry. Please give me some food." The children were so innocent that they gave him the stones, and the saint ate them all.

Grandma's inspiration was so important to me. I spent a great deal of time with her. I was always thinking about God. Always God. "Where is God? Where is God?" When I told grandma about my spiritual experiences, she would say, "If we're always with God, these things will happen. It's natural." The way I grew up was so beautiful.

Grandma and I slept together right in front of the family altar. One morning at three o'clock, something woke me up and I saw a big aura, a big light, around the Krishna statue. At first I thought a thief had come and was shining a flashlight. I asked grandma, "What is this big light?" but she didn't make a fuss about it. Many, many unusual things happened with me and God, and when I told grandma, she never paid attention to them. This was a very important way that she helped me. She was a great soul.

How did that help you?

I didn't think these events were unusual. I thought they were normal. In this country if someone has a powerful experience with God, they tend to make a big deal out of it. Then their ego becomes attached to the event. My grandma taught me that God is taking care of us all and that what we call miracles are normal events when you are in communion with God.

Did you know that other kids weren't having these same experiences?

There weren't any other kids around. It was just grandma and I. I had no interest in other kids. I was very quiet. I would never talk without a reason.

When I was three years old, I started fasting during Shiva Ratri and I performed puja (prayer) to the sun. Grandma taught me to bow down to the sun, because the sun gives us everything. Grandma taught me to do puja three times a day: morning, lunchtime and evening. She taught me about purity and the importance of wearing clean clothes. She was a very pure lady. She'd wake up in the morning and clean the whole house, and she'd burn frankincense. As long as she was alive she did this. You can see how she created a devotional atmosphere.

After a while my elder uncle married and he had four children, and then I lived with their family. I lived with them for a couple of years, and then I was alone with grandma again.

Early Experiences

When I was four years old, I went to a Ramakrishna school. My aunt was assistant headmistress and she taught higher classes there. Most of the time I sat with her at her table. I never thought this was unusual. God was always taking care of me. It was so beautiful.

When we played, we always played spiritual games. For several days we would worship Lakshmi. On other days we would worship Narayana. The boys played football, but we played with God.

When I was four years old, I had an important experience. I was sweeping my house and when I was finished, I threw the broom to the ground. Suddenly, I heard Ramakrishna's voice. When he talked with me he would say "hega," which means "hello" in Bengali. He said, "Hega, why are you throwing that broom? It cleans your floor. Cleanliness is next to Godliness. You should respect your actions all the time." So I bowed down to the broom. He was teaching me to honor and respect everything.

Was Ramakrishna talking to you all the time?

All the time. But I didn't tell my family. I never told other people what was happening to me. Ramakrishna told me, "If you keep your experiences quiet, I will always be there." Once in a while I told my grandma.

When I was five or six years old, I was sleeping with my grandma in our temple that was separate from the house. We had lots of banana trees, and when the bananas were ripe, they kept a whole branch in the temple. One day I was doing puja to Kali and I was crying. It was so beautiful. I was

17

crying for Kali, "Mother, where are you?" I was thinking about how Ramakrishna would say to Kali, "You eat, I eat, you eat, I eat. You take your food and you give me pure devotion." I was doing the same thing. I was playing a game with the Divine Mother. We were feeding each other. I said, "Eat, eat," and was offering her the food, and she ate! She ate and I ate. After that I forgot everything. What I mean is that I went into a state where I wasn't aware of my separate self anymore. Whenever I deeply connect to God, I forget everything.

From the age of six on, I was in that state and I forgot everything. I forgot myself and what was happening to me. Every moment, every hour, every second was like this. During this time my family was irritated with me, because I was so quiet. I took care of my family responsibilities, but I didn't talk and I wasn't attentive at school. I couldn't speak lies and I couldn't listen to lies. It would hurt me inside to listen to lies. No one understood me.

When I was in third grade, my cousins and I were studying with a private tutor, but I didn't want to study. I wanted to think about God. When the tutor asked me a question, I couldn't give the answer. So he said, "Show your hand," and he hit me on my hand. I jumped up and said, "I will never study with this teacher!" and walked out. I never studied with him again, and nobody could force me to. When I experience an inner conviction, no one can change my mind. I studied by myself. Later that teacher grew to respect me.

When I was in the fifth and sixth grade, I was the worst student. I always carried Ramakrishna's picture with me in my sari. I felt connected with Thakur (affectionate name for Ramakrishna) all the time.

Sadhus

When I was eleven years old, I learned that many sadhus (holy men or women) came to our town, and I would sneak out to see them. I met so many holy men and women in my life. Sometimes I went to the mountains to meet them. Other times I found them in the Kali Temple nearby. I never told anybody about these meetings, not even grandma.

I remember when I was in sixth grade, one of my great uncles came from Calcutta. He was a sadhu who never married and spent his whole life wandering from place to place. He never stayed in one place for more than three days. He could read your forehead and tell everything about you. He was a very joyful man. When he saw me, he said, "I don't want to leave you. I will stay here for ten days, and you have to be with me all the time. Wherever I go, you will accompany me." I enjoyed his company, and he told me so many stories. He told me that my first Guru was my grandma. He also said that I would do lots of work for the universe.

My mom asked him to tell the futures of her four children. When he came to me, he wouldn't give an answer, but he said one of her children would go to America and that child would do lots of work for this world. My mother thought he was talking about my brother.

My mom was full of illusion at that time. Maya (the illusion that the material world is the only reality) caught her, because she was so involved in raising her three children that she forgot about God. When she was pregnant with me, she was united with divine consciousness. But after I was born, maya covered her and she forgot about God. My mother prayed for a great child, so a soul came. When she got pregnant with another child, she became consumed with other desires. That is human life.

When Ramakrishna was coming into this world, his mother and father knew who he was. When he was born, they forgot. They started to take care of him like he was a normal child. God is tricky that way. The parents need to forget; otherwise, they could not raise their children.

During that time family and friends saw that when I wanted something, God would bring it to me. So they always wanted me to pray for them. It got to the point that they couldn't think about doing anything without asking me. For instance, my aunt would tell me, "You pray to God so my husband will get a promotion."

Hanging With The Buddha

From the sixth to the eighth grade, I was with Buddha. Every day we had forty-five minutes off from school. During that time I sat in a Buddhist temple and joined in every ceremony. That was one of the reasons why I was not a good student. After school I would visit with a Buddhist family and learn their rituals and culture.

When you say you were with Buddha for two years, do you mean that you talked to him like you did to Ramakrishna?

Yes. When you are born, you have some human tendencies. But if an enlightened teacher is with you all the time telling you stories, then your mind will stay focused on God. So I had a companion all the time. I thought this was normal.

I was not an "A"-student, but I passed. Eighth grade was hard for me. One day I was doing puja, and Ramakrishna told me, "In your last life you did not study and you were sad about that. So in this lifetime you must study."

From the ninth to the eleventh grades, I studied the Muslim religion. Our neighbor was a Muslim, and I was so impressed that he got up every morning at four o'clock to pray that I started to meditate the Muslim way. While my neighbors read their Koran early in the morning, I would sit down with them and meditate.

That sounds similar to the way Ramakrishna experienced many different religious traditions.

I totally followed what Ramakrishna did. He was guiding me.

Family Troubles

When I was fifteen years old, I changed dramatically. I started to meditate automatically and go into samadhi (deep absorption in God). For instance, I would open a book and start reading and then, all of a sudden, I would be gone. I would be eating and then I would be gone. I would lose any sense of a separate self.

My family thought I was abnormal and wondered what had happened to me. Before I had been taking care of my responsibilities and outwardly leading a normal life. Now I was acting strangely. They thought I was crazy.

I can tell you about my first samadhi. As I was slowly going deeper inside, I started to watch the events of my childhood. It was like watching a movie. At the end I came to this event that happened while I was living with my aunt. I was eleven years old. My aunt had a big Kali statue in her house. One day my aunt and uncle left me in the house alone so they could see the dentist. I was so happy! So I started to cry to this big Kali statue up on the shelf, "There is nobody here. Will you please come and see me? Come down and see me!" Now a few feet behind me there was a window with steel rods. At that moment, I looked behind me and I saw a big black cobra. It was over ten feet long and maybe eight inches around. It was unbelievable.

I ran into the other room and closed the door. I put towels under the cracks in the door. I was shaking. I had never seen such a big snake before. After half-an-hour, I went out and saw it was gone. I called some people on the road, and they looked for the snake but couldn't find it. No one believed me. But that fear stayed with me for a couple of years. I would just think about that snake and I would get a fever.

So when I was in samadhi and I came to the end of this movie, this same snake appeared. It said, "When you saw me, you got afraid." That's when I realized that the snake was Kali. I forgot that I had begged her to come to me. I thought, "Oh, you played a trick on me."

When I was sixteen, I couldn't keep any clothing on when I sat down to meditate. I would wrap myself in one cloth for modesty. Everyone thought, "She is our golden girl and she is becoming crazy." By that time they realized that I had been sneaking out to see sadhus. My family was very upset, because they thought these sadhus were doing something to me. Everyone thought I was ruined.

I wanted to be a vegetarian, but every Sunday my family would eat chicken. One Sunday when all my aunts and uncles were at the table, I said, "I don't want to eat chicken. I don't want to eat fish or eggs or meat." They all forced me to eat. I took one bite of the chicken and I fainted. Then they knew not to force me to eat anymore.

Eventually I didn't eat with others of my family because they weren't vegetarian. I ate with my grandma. It was very hard for all of us when I stopped eating with them. They were always yelling at me. One night I was in samadhi all evening. I was sitting under a mosquito net lost in samadhi when my uncle turned on the light and shook me and yelled, "What are you doing?" I started crying, "Guru, Guru, Guru," and ran away. I used to wear my hair in braids. When I started crying, all my braids flew open. I became Kali. I was very ferocious. My golden bracelets opened on my wrists. From that time on, I stopped braiding my hair and wearing ornaments.

Eventually I couldn't eat food any more, because I was in deep meditation all the time. This was when I was fifteen, sixteen and seventeen years old. I was losing weight, and everyone was worried. At least twenty-two people in my family were living together: uncles, aunts, children and servants. You can imagine how much food there was every evening. Rice and dahl, vegetables and fish. One day everyone was talking about me, and they were very upset because I wasn't eating. So that night I went into the kitchen and started eating the food with both hands. There were three big pots of dahl, vegetables and rice. I ate and ate and ate. Finally I finished all the food for twenty-two people. After that they thought I was totally crazy.

That must have scared them.

Yes. They wanted to give me electric shock treatments.

So they didn't think it was a miracle?

No, they thought I was out of my mind. I did unusual things. I was eating with the dogs and cats. I saw everything as divine. Every being was divine.

When Ramakrishna was crying for the Divine Mother and was totally crazy, Mathur Baba protected him. Otherwise, other people would have beaten him.

Was your grandma your protector?

For some time. But ultimately the family let me do what I wanted.

I can't tell you stories about college, because I don't remember. I don't remember taking my examinations. I had one or two pure friends, and they could relate to me. It was a beautiful stage. I went here and there. Words came from my mouth automatically, and people felt inspired. A big group started to gather around me.

The Devotees Come

After college I went to see my mother in Gauhati while I was still in this state of consciousness. By God's grace there was a big Durga Temple where my mother lived. The people there were very spiritual, and I was so happy. I read the *Chandi Path* (teaching story about the Divine Mother) every day. By that time I had lots of followers. Sometimes I was acting so strangely that my mother couldn't tolerate it. She had forgotten her divinity.

Trailinga Swami came to my meditations often and he helped me a lot. I didn't know who he was. Then Trailinga Swami's disciples started coming to see me. At another time Shubas Bose's followers came from Calcutta to ask me for advice. My mother got so mad. She said, "Who is she that all these people are coming to take her advice?" My

27

mother did some bad things to me. She used me for her selfish desires.

A famous saint named Ram Nath Aghori Baba, who was 280 years old, came to the Kamakhya Temple. My mom told me, "We are going to see Ram Nath Aghori Baba. You have to stay home. We don't want you involved with any more sadhus." Everyone went to see him. I stayed home and went into deep meditation. Suddenly I noticed a beautiful incense and datura flower smell. Everything was hugging me. I woke up and thought, "What's going on?" I heard Ram Nath's voice say, "You have to come and see me." I said, "I have no money. How will I go?" and he said, "Go to the closet, and inside the white shirt there are fifteen rupees." So I got up and went to the closet and, sure enough, in my uncle's shirt pocket I found the fifteen rupees. I ran out of the house. I didn't care that the house was open or that a thief might get in. When I went outside, a rickshaw was waiting there. Isn't that amazing? He took me to the bus station. The bus was there, even though it wasn't scheduled to be there. I took two buses and went to the Kamakhya Temple. When I arrived, Ram Nath Aghori Baba was just leaving. He saw me and he said, "You came!" Then he blessed me and said, "This Shree Maa is an example of truth for the Kali Yuga." He turned to the crowd of people bidding him good-bye and said, "Now you must take care of this world."

After that meeting, I can't remember where I went. I was walking, walking, walking. Many people knew me. They said,

"She was sitting here in samadhi. She was in this temple in samadhi."

What did that feel like?

My mind was with God. Wherever they took me or wherever I was called, I went. One time I suddenly found myself on top of a mountain. There was only one saint there alone, and he was crying when he saw me. He said, "I was calling you and you came!" I didn't say one word to him. I went to his temple, and there was a big havan kund (sacred fire). He was a follower of Chinnamasta, Mother Kali. He fed me and did puja to me. When the puja was complete, I came out of samadhi.

The Kamakhya Temple

During the Mother Kamakhya festival, the temple is closed for three days. Saints come from all over India to sit and meditate outside the temple. I closed my door for those three days. I didn't eat or go to the bathroom. One day a saint was crying for Mother in the Durga Temple. Suddenly some energy took me out of my room to this saint, who was in deep meditation in the temple. He opened the door and said, "Bhagavati Maa! You came!"

Did you hear the call?

Yes. I heard the call.

Every moment there was something. I was in the cremation grounds also.

So you would just find yourself someplace?

No, I had no sense of self.

You were one with everything?

Yes. No self. Many Buddhist monks came from Tibet and wanted to take me there. Then a big movement started around me, so I ran away.

During one of the three-day Mother Kamakhya festivals, I was fasting and not even taking a drop of water. I was in the nearby Bhairavi Temple, and many people had come with me. I heard later that many people did puja to me while I was in samadhi. Everyone thought I was going to leave my body, because if you are in samadhi for too long, you can't keep your body. But I wasn't in samadhi constantly. I would be in samadhi for eight or twelve hours and then I would come back again. I wasn't eating much at all. Many sadhus were saying that if she keeps this up, she will not stay in her body anymore.

After three days the door of the Kamakhya Temple opened, and I woke up. There were thousands of people waiting to go into the temple. I thought I would like to go inside the temple, too. When the temple door opened, I saw a big light and I fainted. Two other devotees and a sadhu saw me, and

they took me to the havan kund and gave me milk and warmed me by the fire.

After that I was very famous in that area. I started to go there less, because people knew me and demanded things. But that time was very beautiful.

One day the wife of a doctor came to me and said, "My husband saw you in a dream. In the dream it explained where you were. He is crying, and you have to come and see him." It was far away, but I went with her because I inwardly recognized her husband, who was half-paralyzed. I stayed with him a month. I loved him. He could not leave me, and I could not leave him. I had a big Shiva lingam (symbol of the God Shiva) sent from Banaras and I established it there. It was very beautiful. The devotion was uplifting.

Then I started going to different devotees' houses to do puja, and people would gather. One time, late at night, we were walking back from a devotee's house. We saw a man with a jeep and asked him if he would give us a lift. With God's grace he took us. When he got home, he couldn't sleep all night because in his dream he saw Mother Kali, and she said, "You took me in your jeep, but you didn't recognize me?" At five in the morning, he came back to the house where I was staying. I was in samadhi. I was often in samadhi. He came and bowed down and left. After that he became a great devotee.

It was a beautiful time. When I came out of samadhi, so many Sanskrit shlokas (verses) came out of my mouth and I talked so much.

Meeting Swami

While in meditation one night, I suddenly heard Mother tell me, "You have to go to Bakreshwar and meet Satyananda." When I came out of samadhi, I told everybody. In those days various people's names would come to me during meditation, and then they would come to see me. So when I mentioned the name Satyananda, one devotee said, "Oh Mother, Satyananda will come to see you. You don't have to go to him." Later I went back into meditation, and the voice said again that I should go to Bakreshwar and meet him. I saw a vision of Swamiji coming down from heaven with his two hands raised in blessing, and he was chanting the "Devi Suktam" from the *Chandi*. He came down and he went in front of the Shiva statue, and then he merged into it...

(Just then Swami walked into the room to look for something. This was the only time he did so during these interviews with Shree Maa.)

We were just talking about you, and here you are!

See!

(Swami says nothing, smiles and leaves.)

When I woke up, I said, "I have to go to Bakreshwar. Where is Bakreshwar?" and one devotee said, "I know where it is. It's near Calcutta. There is a famous temple of the Divine Mother there."

So a week later, we went to Calcutta. Then we took a bus to Bakreshwar and arrived there at evening time. The next morning I woke up from my meditation. Mother's energy was pulling me, and it was so powerful that it forced me to start running. I stopped running when I reached the gate of a small temple at the far side of the bathing tank, underneath a great banyan tree. I saw a man opening a lock to the gate of the temple and told him, "I would like to see Satyananda." He immediately went inside and said to Swamiji, "You have to see this Mother outside. She is something." When he entered into the temple, he forgot to lock the gate, so I entered along with all of my devotees. Without waiting for anyone's permission, we sat down in the temple and began to meditate. Swami was just preparing to sit for his morning worship and did not see me as I entered. But after a little more than half-an-hour, I heard Swami's voice call loudly, "Get out of here!" I woke up out of meditation and took a marigold and a sweet from his altar and went to meet him. I recognized him from when I saw him in my vision during my previous meditation. I put the flower on his head. We looked at each other. Tears were flowing down our cheeks. I put the sweet in his mouth and then I turned around and went back to Calcutta.

Why did you turn around and leave? Why didn't you stay?

I knew he would come to me. Some time later I was in Vashishta's house and I remained in samadhi for two days. People said, "We have to interrupt her samadhi, or she will leave her body." Everyone was chanting, because they wanted to wake me up. There was a big group. On the third day, I woke up in the afternoon, and just at that moment Swami came. Vashishta was hugging him and crying, "She said you would come! She said you would come! But she's upstairs in her room, sitting in samadhi." Swamiji said, "She will come down soon."

After meeting Swami lots of miracles occurred. I started performing big pujas with thousands of people. All of Calcutta came. I went to many different places: Bangladesh, the Himalayas, Nepal, all over India. I wanted to wake everybody up.

Every Moment Is A Miracle

There is one thing that I want to tell you. Every moment of my life is a celebration. To you my life may seem like a beautiful miracle, but I feel this is the natural life of a human being. This is natural, not a miracle. When we live with truth and purity every second, every moment is a miracle. You are living with God. You are God! Isn't it beautiful?

We came to this world to do God's work. We came to this world to do our real duty. G-O-D: Go On Duty. With God's grace scientists are doing so many wonderful things. But they don't know who is really doing these things. They think they are doing them alone. Therefore, it is now the time on earth we call the Kali Yuga or the Dark Age. We think we have created this whole thing. We think "I, I, I."

But now I am playing a game with you guys to make everything divine.

What kind of game?

A divine game. Someday we will go to our real home.

When you know you are a child of God, that is surrender. If you don't know who you are, it is hard to surrender. Your heart has to be soft. If you remember you are a child of God, you will become purer day by day. First comes simplicity, later comes respect. When you think, "I am a child of God," respect will come to you in every moment.

Is that similar to having a relationship with God like you had with Ramakrishna?

I was not only with Ramakrishna; I was with everybody. I would not pick up a flower without God's name. Mother Earth is giving all this to us. It is Mother Earth's prasad (gift). Every morning I wake up early and I bow to the sun and I bow to Mother Earth. She gives us so much. She gives us divine prasad. Mother Earth gives all nourishment to us, and we don't give her respect. When I walk I say God's name during every step, and she can feel that. She can feel someone doing something for her, protecting her. You have to be that way every moment.

My grandma told me to wake up early in the morning, look in the mirror and bow down to myself. It's very simple, but we make it complicated.

It's hard to remember.

It's not hard. Every day you need to brush your teeth. In the same way, every day you have to think, "I am a child of God."

During the time on earth we call the Satya Yuga or the age of truth, everyone knew he or she was a child of God and that they had come to take care of Mother Earth. Everyone was divine in the age of truth. Now we are destroying Mother Earth.

Always pray to God to get His grace. If we think we are a child of God all the time, our actions will become divine. Automatically everything will come to us.

Does one ask the Divine Mother for grace, like we'd ask our own mother for a birthday present?

Yes. I ask her for devotion and wisdom all the time. When you have pure devotion, pure knowledge will come.

It sounds so simple.

It is very simple. That is why we need to do spiritual practices, to remind ourselves to remember divinity all the time. But performing spiritual practices is no substitute for leading a spiritual life. Everyone is God. Mother is everywhere. That's why I like to keep pictures of Gods and Goddesses around me. It's fun.

But what you are listening to now is nothing. Every second has divinity. It never ends.

2

God Will Give You Everything You Desire

After completing our second interview, I was shocked to find that, due to technical problems, none of the interview had been recorded. I was crestfallen. Since interviewing Shree Maa was such a rare privilege, I felt that something precious had been lost.

Shree Maa says everything happens for a beautiful reason, so I reflected on what the purpose of this event could have been. As I reconstructed the interview for this chapter, the answer became clear to me. Because I included my personal reactions to Shree Maa's answers in this chapter, subsequent interviews, and therefore the entire book, took on a more personal dimension. I hope this addition made the wisdom of this book more accessible to the reader.

Following are the highlights of that interview.

Early in the conversation I asked Shree Maa,

How can someone who reads this book or sees you once a year at one of your programs have a relationship with you?

Shree Maa gave me a piercing look and said, "If they call for me sincerely in their heart, I will know." Then she paused for a second and said, "I am the Mother of the Universe. I am with everyone."

It was such an astonishing statement that I was shocked. I had never heard her make this kind of direct declaration about her state of consciousness. People will say to her that she is a saint or an enlightened being, and she won't disagree, but she doesn't make pronouncements about herself.

When Shree Maa says that she is the Mother of the Universe, she doesn't mean she is the only Mother of the Universe. According to Shree Maa, all of us are God. Some of us realize that, and some of us don't. According to Shree Maa, there are a number of other beings presently living on this planet who have attained her level of realization.

Some may think her statement to be egotistical, but Shree Maa seems to have little or no ego. She is the most humble person I have ever known. Once when walking in the front door of a house, a few people were sitting on the floor, blocking her way. Rather than ask them to get up, she began to walk around the outside of the house so that she could enter through the back door.

If you spend time with Shree Maa, you can't help but see that many miracles occur around her. For instance, two days before this interview, I heard the caretaker for the land she lives on tell Shree Maa that there hadn't been enough rain this winter. He was concerned the ashram might experience a water shortage. Shree Maa said she would pray for rain that afternoon. That evening it rained hard and continued raining solidly for the next five days. One may think, "Well, it could have rained anyway," and, of course, that is true. So when miracles occur, you're never quite sure what is happening.

Getting back to the interview, after Shree Maa said that she was the Mother of the Universe, I collected myself for a moment and then replied,

That's amazing. It's hard to understand what you just said. So if someone calls to you, you will hear their call? What if a hundred people call to you at the same time? Will you hear all of them?

Shree Maa replied matter of factly, "Yes."

Sometimes Shree Maa will say something so profound, with such a penetrating look in her eyes, that it's hard to continue asking questions. I just want to sit in the profound peace that I feel. Being in Shree Maa's presence usually creates an altered state, but sometimes she seems to turn things up a notch, and then it gets really interesting. This was one of those times. I struggled to ask my next question.

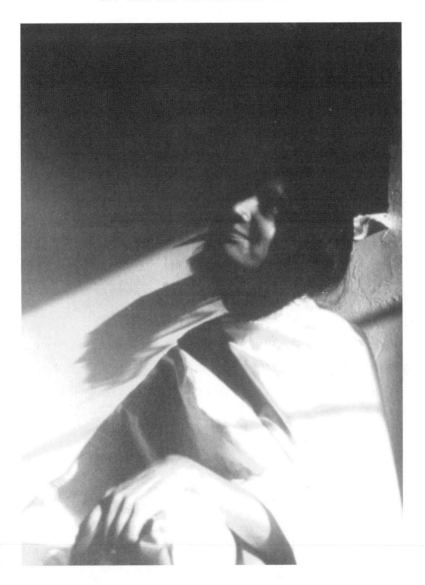

Do you hear specifically what they are saying to you?

Of course!

I'm sure I should have followed up on these questions, but I wasn't sure how. I certainly wasn't comfortable asking her, "What does that mean that you are the Mother of the Universe?"

I asked her some questions about life after death that she seemed not to want to discuss. She did say, "The universe is much bigger than you can imagine."

I was also very happy to hear her say about death, "When you get there, I'll show you what to do."

At one point she said, "God will give you everything you desire. Isn't that true for you?"

I thought about my life and saw that, although it had been difficult, it was true that most of what I wanted I eventually received, with some important exceptions. I replied,

Well, yes, mostly. But there are lots of things I desired that I didn't get.

Tell me one.

Well, at one point I went to L.A. to create conscious television programs, and although I did create them, they weren't successful.

You weren't ready. It wasn't the right time. Maybe when you are ready, you will create television programs about God.

So is it that we get all our desires fulfilled and then we don't want them any more?

No, because fulfilling some desires just creates more desires.

Then she surprised me with a statement from another galaxy. "You are with me twenty-four hours a day. I can't get rid of you." She said this while laughing. She was saying something very important and at the same time she was kidding with me.

I was floored. It's true that I think about her often, but certainly not most of the time.

I replied,

Even when I sleep?

Yes.

But there are many times when I'm not thinking about you.

That's your mind. I'm talking about your soul.

I was left to ponder these incredible assertions. My soul is with her twenty-four hours a day. She is the Mother of the Universe. She'll show me around after I die. What am I to make of all this?

3

MY HOME IS EVERYWHERE

That was really something, wasn't it? I taped that whole interview, and nothing came out.

God has His plan. There is nothing to worry about.

In the first interview, when you told your life story you said that you were always talking with God.

I was born with God's name and I grew up with God's name. My mind was not focused on this world. God gave me that consciousness. God does everything.

So you were born that way.

I was born that way and grew up that way. I can't think about anything that doesn't contain divinity.

You can't even imagine it being different than that?

No, I can't. But you guys were raised differently. You were molded in a materialistic way. Your parents weren't involved with God, although they knew a little bit about God. In this culture you feel you have to do everything yourself and you

have to be involved in the materialistic world. In India we are taught that spirituality comes first, then we do our work in the world. But we do it for God. This is the difference between the East and West.

The Western countries are new countries. India is an old country. It is steeped in Godliness. It is God's purpose that the West is the way it is and the East is the way it is. Now you can see that the whole world is uniting. God is making oneness. It is so beautiful! In the future the whole world will be very peaceful.

Everyone comes to this world for a different purpose. Everyone comes with their own karma, their own samskaras (tendencies). It is very interesting.

Our upbringing was very different from yours.

That is changing. Now different kinds of children are coming to this planet, and you will see that they will make a contribution to this world.

You once said that a saint had told you that great spiritual children will be born again on earth starting in 1985.

Yes. They will change this planet.

I know that we were raised differently in this country, but how can we talk to God?

If you want God, you have to use willpower to reach Him.

You have to make that your goal and not be distracted by anything.

Right. Also faith is important. You need faith.

How does somebody have faith?

Not everyone is able to have faith. Everyone has their own samskaras, their own karma. Not everyone will realize their divinity in this lifetime. It is a cycle of life, a cycle of karma. It takes many lifetimes of purification to come to the place where you have real faith.

What about someone who reads this book or comes to see you at a program and who really wants to know God?

Most people are just curious. They come to see me to enjoy themselves. Of five thousand people, maybe one soul is touched and feels the desire to change.

Is that right, only one person?

If one soul is touched and wants to change, that is great!

So we are talking about very few people.

Yes, very few people. In the first class compartment, you find first class people. Therefore, in first class you find very few people. God is first class (laughing)!

Do you think that those few people can change the whole world?

They can change the world to some degree, but you can't say that the whole world will change. If you can change those around you — yourself, your wife, your children — if you make them divine, isn't that beautiful? If every individual did that, it would be wonderful.

For example, you are a doctor, a psychologist, and people come to you and love you so much, because through your inspiration and instruction they can change their lives.

But I want to help greater numbers of people than I do now.

Why greater numbers first? You can't jump to the roof. You have to go step by step.

I'm jumping ahead of myself?

Yes. That's the problem with people in Western countries (laughing). They like to jump all the time (laughing). They want everything to be ready-made.

So if a person reads this book or they meet you in person...

Some people are ready and they get it immediately. Some people are thirsty and when they see a pure soul, they are touched. But even if they don't feel anything, I give them a blessing. I give a blessing to everyone to change his or her life.

What does this blessing do?

If they are suffering, it is a cure. It will help them. It will reduce their karma.

Is that right?

Of course, it will create some effect. This is a cycle of relationships over many lifetimes with the whole universe.

So if they see you just once, they will get relief from their troubles?

Of course, of course. I can't take away their whole karma, but some karma will be reduced. It's like the story of the thief and the sadhu. The sadhu was walking in the forest and he stepped on a thorn. While he was taking the thorn out, a thief came to that same spot and instead of getting stuck by a thorn, he found a gold coin.

When the sadhu got back to his Guru, he said, "What is this? I have been meditating for years and making a contribution to society, while that thief has been lying and stealing. Why did he get a gold coin and I got a thorn?"

The Guru said, "Today you were supposed to be hanged, but because of the good karma you got from the deeds you have performed in this life, you escaped with the prick of a thorn. Today the thief was supposed to become a king, but because of his selfishness he only got one gold coin."

Will people also get a blessing just from reading this book?

Of course. Many people were touched by reading my biography.

If someone reads this book or sees you in person and then they pray to you in their heart?

They will receive a blessing. Everything will come to them. It doesn't matter what desire someone wants from God. Some people are praying for money, some for happiness or pleasure, some for God Himself. But all those who pray are praying with faith. When people pray with faith, I am sure they are praying to God and God will hear.

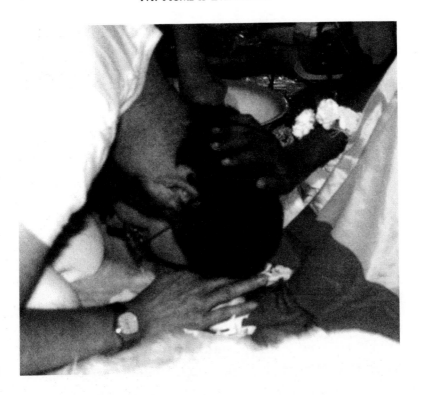

So just the act of prayer creates a blessing.

Yes!

Is praying to you the same as praying to God?

Yes. There is no doubt about that. The love of the Guru is the same as the love of God. Both are free from selfishness. Any time you pray without selfishness, all that is divine will respond.

Will you hear specifically what they are saying?

53

Yes, without a doubt.

You said this same thing in the last interview, and I find it so amazing. It's hard to understand what you just said with my mind.

It is very difficult to understand from your head. Therefore, we always say in our country to live in your heart. If you want to change your life, you can do it very quickly with your heart.

In the Western countries, we are usually coming from our head?

Yes. Because you were raised in a materialistic way, you use your head a lot. That's why I love computers. God is so tricky. He said, "These people are too intellectual. We have to change their world." So God made the computer. Why did God make the computer? When you are using your mind too much, you want more, more, more. The unfocused mind tends to jump from one thing to the next.

Computers are making people one-pointed, calm, quiet and meditative. Go to a business in Silicon Valley and watch the people there. Then go to a factory or a construction site. You will see a difference. The computer people are very sweet, calm and quiet. They are focusing their minds. Look and judge for yourself. Computers are helping to make this world more peaceful.

In this country so many of us are stuck in our heads...

But they can change their life very quickly with their hearts.

In India spirituality is the heart of the culture, and all activities spring from it. Many of you came from India in previous lifetimes and you understand this kind of spirituality. You came to the West to make oneness, to bring the East and West together.

What is your reason for coming to the United States?

This whole universe is mine. Where God sends me, that is where I go. For you, this is the United States. For me it is not the United States. For me, it is home.

Is every place your home?

Yes.

Is it a good practice to have a picture of you and talk to that picture?

If that is your desire. For me it is good to look at a picture of Ramakrishna, because he guided me from my childhood. My heart is his heart. I am He and I am She. We are the same. Yet I like to have his picture in my room and look at him and respect him. I like to have pictures of Gods and Goddesses in my room, because I feel divinity from them. But you have to make your own personal relationship with God.

You have said that God gives us everything.

Yes.

Yet most people feel they haven't gotten everything they wanted. They didn't get the job they wanted or the boyfriend they longed for.

When we are really doing our duty, our purpose for being on earth, what will happen?

Everything comes to us?

Yes (laughing)! It is very simple.

But we don't always know what God wants us to do.

If we think G-O-D, Go On Duty, we will know right away.

Are you saying if we want to do God's work, we will know what to do?

Yes. That's why we came here.

We can talk to God, right?

Do you talk to God?

Yes.

For what purpose do you talk to God?

Sometimes because I'm confused and...

And you get answers, right?

Yes.

You see (laughing). Why did God give us twenty-four hours? It has a purpose. We spend eight hours for work for the world, eight hours for personal time and eight hours for God. But how many people spend eight hours thinking about God? Mostly people are thinking "I, I, I." Maybe once in a while, for one second, they think about God. During special times, like when they are suffering, they might remember God. We are human beings. This is the highest birth for this earth. But still we are fighting and showing discrimination. This is sad. We need to change (laughing). Ninety-nine percent of the people need to change. But everything is all right. The earth is a very difficult place to live. There is so much duality here.

You once said that there was a ratio of ninety percent duality to ten percent non-duality on this planet.

Yes. Ninety percent duality. Of all the planets with human life, this planet has the most duality.

Wow, what a place to be living (laughing)!

Therefore, if you perform spiritual practices, you won't come back for a long time. Now you are thinking, "Oh, this pleasure and pain, it's nice." But when you leave your body, you'll feel free and you'll say, "I'm going home!" If you perform good karma here, you will go to a beautiful place and you will not want to come back. But when it's time to come back and teach people, you will.

The important thing is to remember God all the time. Creation is beautiful! (Laughing) The whole universe is beautiful!

In the last interview, you said that the universe is bigger than we can imagine.

That's right! We are little bugs in this universe.

And you are in touch with it all?

Yes (laughing). It is a drama, a game. I am playing a divine game, but I am not playing the game to get name or fame.

Is part of the game for you to act like a human being?

Yes, yes. In a divine way.

To show us how it can be done?

Right.

Thank you very much for this.

Thank you. I appreciate your questions. This is good for you.

Yes. Very good. Here's another question. What is the Divine Mother?

You wanted to know who the Divine Mother was, so we gave you some instructions to reach Her, and now you are following them step by step.

So you can experience the Divine Mother if you perform spiritual practices?

Yes. That is important. When you perform spiritual practices, you will experience the Divine Mother. If you don't wash your eating utensils every day, what will happen? You have to wash your utensils every day to eat.

So we are the utensils?

Hey (laughing)!

4

The Guru Is Learning, Too

Could you tell the story you once told me about the time you
wanted your favorite snack and you ran out of it?

I was in school at that time and, as I said before, I was
always sneaking out to see sadhus. Whenever I heard that
a sadhu was passing through our town, I would visit him.
One winter night I was going to see one of these sadhus,
but before leaving I wanted to have a hot drink and eat a
salty snack called crunchy-munchy. We would always drink
something hot and eat the crunchy-munchy in the evening
in wintertime, but this time there wasn't any left. I was
disappointed.

Just before I was going to leave to see the sadhu, a big
storm arrived, but I went anyway. When I arrived, there were
about two hundred people meditating very quietly. I was the
last person to arrive. I sat down and started to meditate.
After forty-five minutes, I suddenly felt something land in my
lap. I opened my eyes with a start and saw that it was the
crunchy-munchy I wanted. It was a big package. I said, "Oh,

my God," and I was really impressed. The saint knew I wanted that snack.

After that I looked at him for a long time and then I gave everybody some of the snack as prasad. Then I ate a little bit myself in order to dissolve my desire. I learned on that day not to get attached to my desires. That perception came from the Guru's action. He gave me that teaching. It was very sweet.

When I offered everybody the prasad, the saint was still in samadhi. He woke up out of samadhi when I finished giving out the prasad. It was about 11:30 PM. He started crying and crying. He called to me, "Maa, Maa, Maa, come to me." He told me to sit down next to him and asked me to sing. I started singing, "Jago, Durga. Wake up, Divine Mother." He was crying and he could not sit still. He was crying and crying. He kept saying, "You wake up, you wake up!" He was waking me up. He was reminding me who I was. From that day, I started to recall my past memories.

From past lifetimes you mean?

Yes. And I started to get detached from my family. I was realizing who I was and what was going on with me. It was a big change.

So it was a turning point.

Yes, it was very beautiful.

You were saying that whenever you had a desire...

It would always come. Like yesterday. When I was cleaning my altar, I was thinking, "Oh please, somebody bring me a rose (laughing). That would make me so happy. Maybe I should call Parvati to bring some roses." You won't believe it (laughing), but I looked behind me and Roger was standing there with roses. I hugged him and hugged him and said, "I was just talking to Shiva about roses, and you brought roses!" It was so sweet.

Does it always happen that way?

Yes, it always happens that way. It happens for everybody if you have a pure heart and are thinking pure thoughts. God will be living with you always. It never fails.

So when you have that kind of relationship with God, these things always happen?

Yes. You are trying to be pure, Mahavir (my spiritual name), and you will get that also. You will get and you will give. You will have the ability to give. The most important things are truth and simplicity, devotion and wisdom, simplicity and faith. They all go together.

What do you mean by simplicity?

When you are devotional, you are uncomplicated.

That makes sense. So you were saying that the Guru helped you wake up and remember who you were. Before that experience did you know who you were?

No. Before, I knew I was a child of God. I always knew that. And I always lived with God.

So you always had that.

My whole childhood. But when you live in samsara (duality), with a family, they have so much attachment to worldly things. Sometimes their worldly attachments make you attached.

Is that part of the human drama?

Yes. It's the drama. For example, the last time I went to India many members of my family came to see me. I hadn't seen them in a long time, but I felt that they hadn't changed. They got old, but they were the same as before.

No wisdom?

They had wisdom, but they were bound by maya (attachment to the world). They didn't realize they were instruments of God. They didn't know who they were.

It was interesting for me to watch my uncle. On one hand, he was sharing spiritual knowledge with all my devotees. On the other hand, he was bound by maya. I said to him, "You are sharing so much wisdom with these people. So why are

64

you so sad?" He said, "We know this wisdom and we would like to live this way, but it's very hard to do." The family environment binds them to maya. If they did satsangha (gathering of spiritual friends) on a regular basis or went to see saints, they could change.

Is that why it's so important to have satsangha?

Yes, it's very important.

You know in the West we were raised with the idea that God may punish you if you don't do the right thing. We were raised with a fear of sin and hell.

God never punishes. God only gives us whatever we want. Our ego creates the suffering.

That's the opposite of what most people think.

Yes. Why would God punish you? Why are you blaming God?

So we're not taking responsibility for creating our own suffering?

Yes. This is not the right attitude. When we are not perfect, we create suffering. We create our karma and we suffer. Why blame God?

A lot of people feel alone in this world and they don't think there is a supreme divinity.

65

Because they are identified with their ego. Therefore, lots of people think that way. If they let go of their selfishness, they would know that God is here. If they live with pure love, they will know that.

It's so hard to have pure love.

In Western countries it is very hard to feel pure love. It was not that way on this planet before. This is a Dark Age for human beings.

I think many people are afraid of God.

Because of ego (laughing). They don't want to lose themselves.

So that's the real fear. Because even I'm afraid of you sometimes.

Why?

Well, I think you're right. I think it is a fear of losing my ego, because my ego does dissolve to some degree when I'm around you. So that's what it is?

Yes.

Is a real Guru the same as God?

The real Guru is Shiva.

And a real Guru in the body is the same as Shiva?

If he has pure knowledge. If the Guru is showing the divine path, he is a real Guru. In this life everyone wants to be a Guru; nobody wants to be a disciple. My feeling is that we are all disciples, always. We are learning every moment.

Even the Gurus are learning?

Of course! We are disciples of God and we are learning all the time. As long as this body is on earth, we are learning every moment. Learning never ends.

So even an enlightened Guru is learning?

Of course we are learning. Always.

What is a disciple's responsibility to a Guru?

Respect. When you have respect, pure love will come to you. When you are emulating the Guru's behavior, it is like a garland. You are making a pure, shining garland of truth and love.

All a disciple has to do is respect the Guru, and everything unfolds from there?

Yes, but you have to pick the right Guru.

How can one tell who a true Guru is?

A true Guru speaks the truth and he doesn't discriminate. You can feel if someone is a true Guru, (laughing) if you are the right kind of person.

So you have to be the right disciple.

We have a saying, "You can see thousands of Gurus in this world, but it is hard to find one true disciple." Isn't that true?

Well...

Well?

It seems like there aren't many true Gurus.

That is true, also. But every Guru gives something. Even if you get a little knowledge, you should respect her and be grateful. You shouldn't judge her.

So you can get something even from an unenlightened Guru.

Yes. Even from your father or your mother or your family. It's all a relationship with the Earth Mother.

So everyone is a Guru, if you see it correctly.

Uhum.

Does everybody have a Guru somewhere who is helping them and guiding them?

Not everybody, but whoever wants one.

Whoever wants one will have one?

Yes. Everybody should want one, but how many people do?

Does a Guru have a responsibility to his disciple?

Of course. If a Guru gives a disciple initiation, it is a big responsibility. You have to take care of the disciple for many lifetimes.

Does the Guru have to keep coming back until all of his disciples are enlightened?

Yes.

That is a big responsibility.

I heard somewhere that you cannot be free without the Guru's grace.

I would say without God's grace.

So when you want a Guru and you call out for one, you will get one?

Without doubt, you will get one. If you call in a true way, the Guru will come. There is no question about it.

You once said to me that if you take one step toward God, God will take ten steps towards you.

Yes, that's true.

You were quoting Ramakrishna the other night as saying that God can come down and dwell in a human body. How is it possible that God, who is everything, could be contained in a body, which is one thing?

When the divine spirit comes into a body and He shows this to the universe, what happens? He is with everything. He is with everybody. He shows his divinity. Look at Ramakrishna. Where is he not? He is everywhere, he is everywhere.

So what a gift! He's saying, "Hey, look, I'm here. You can see me!"

What a gift of divinity.

At one point in Ramakrishna's life, he was distraught because the Divine Mother wasn't appearing to him. He was going to kill himself if she didn't show up. Yet he was the Divine Mother; he was God himself.

When we take birth, we come into this body with its five elements. The body is not eternal. There are five organs and five senses. When we take this body on earth, our actions are different. We forget ourselves when we live in this maya, this duality. Then a certain time comes to wake up.

Ramakrishna had that moment, and I had that moment. For example, when I was living with my family after college, many people were coming to my house. Some came because they saw me in a dream or they came intuitively.

My family was so angry. They thought, "Who is she that these people are coming to take advice from her?" Especially my mother was very angry that these people were coming and she was worried that they might hurt me. But actually her ego was popping out. I was unaffected. I tolerated her ego, but one day I got angry.

With your mom?

Not with my mom, with God. So I took an axe and I was talking with Mother Kali. I said, "Why are you making them full of ego. Why? You are going to die today." Then I started hitting my head with the axe. I said to Kali, "Either you show your divinity or you will die today. I will kill this five-element body." I was hitting my head with the axe and then I fainted. My family got scared. They called the police and said I was trying to commit suicide.

Were you bleeding?

No. Nothing happened to me. When they saw what I did and that I was not affected by it, they knew that a real miracle had occurred. My mother was amazed and she bowed down to me.

That evening I left home. I walked and walked and I finally arrived at the Kamakhya Temple. I was going to jump into the Brahmaputra River. That night there was a big storm with a lot of rain, and it was very dark. I tried to jump into the river, but suddenly I saw a bright light. The bright light pushed me away from the river. Then a sound came from the sky and it said, "You can't leave. You have lots to do! I AM YOU!" I fell down on the stones, and the light dissolved, and I fainted. When I woke up, I was in the temple. Someone took me there. I saw that they were doing puja to me and offering me milk. It was so beautiful. Isn't that beautiful?

Yes. They gave you pure love.

That happens to everybody. When you really cry for God, divinity will come to you.

That's beautiful.

After that my family never said anything to me. They didn't see me for many years.

So the same thing happened to you that happened to Ramakrishna.

That happens to anyone who really cries for God. It happened to St. Francis and it happened to Mother Theresa. She was in the West, but she couldn't open her heart there. Somebody was calling her, and she left and went to India. You will see this in the life of every divine being.

How can you make divisions in this world and pretend that we are different people? We are one family. Wherever God wants us, we go. Isn't it beautiful?

Yes. Very beautiful.

You cannot discriminate and say, "I am a Christian, I am a Muslim, I am a Hindu."

So in the case of Ramakrishna and you also, when God comes to the earth in a human body, at a certain point they wake up.

When the right time comes.

Were you also awake before that, but in a different way?

Yes.

That's fascinating. You know, when you said that when you cry to God for something, He will respond, I was thinking that I prayed to God for a Guru to come into my life, and here you are sitting in front of me.

God gives to us step by step (laughing). It can't be like an electric step, though.

Like an escalator?

Yes (laughing).

This is so amazing. You start talking like this and it's hard for me to keep asking you questions. The feeling is so powerful.

I do have another question. What makes you the happiest?

I am always happy. When you always live with divinity, you are always happy. It makes me even happier when my children are happy.

It does seem like you are joyful all the time. It's so wonderful to see. So many people aren't happy on this planet. But there is something difficult about being in a body and being bound by the five elements, isn't there?

Yes.

Is that painful for you?

This is just drama (laughing).

You don't take it seriously.

Just think that while you're here, you are an actor and then you'll go home. Be the best actor you can and realize it's a play.

It's so easy for us to get caught up in the play and think it's real.

If you think you are an actor, you won't get caught up too much (laughing).

Saying mantras (Sanskrit words used for meditation) seems to help.

Yes. Therefore, we have different tools to help remember who we are. Meditation, sadhana (spiritual practices), mantra, satsangha.

Just to remind ourselves. I like that way of looking at it.

There is something that happens to me frequently that I wanted to ask you about. One day I was playing the ektar (Indian stringed instrument) in the temple and the string suddenly went out of tune. I thought maybe that was a message. So I stopped playing and I walked outside. At that moment you were just about to go somewhere in the car and you invited me to come along, which was something I really wanted to do. So that was...

That was the message.

It seems like that happens a lot.

When you have a strong connection with a Guru, that will happen a lot. You are becoming pure. We are one soul, we are one soul. We are always connected.

So as you become more pure, you can feel the truth of that connection more?

Yes. We are becoming one. It's beautiful. It is just like the story I told you of wanting to eat the crunchy-munchy. I am a pure soul, and he is a pure soul and he knew right away what I wanted.

So when the ego decreases...

As your ego dissolves, the connection grows.

And I don't have to be around you physically for that connection to happen, right?

No, no. You can be anywhere in the world. Anywhere.

That's what I was feeling.

My Indian children still have a deep relationship with me. They see me and they feel me.

They still see you and feel you, even though they are on the other side of the world.

Yes. It's just pure devotion.

5

A Story About Shree Maa

After knowing Shree Maa from a distance for two years, I finally got a chance to spend some extended time with her. She and Swami were going to spend the summer traveling around the United States offering musical programs, and I had the opportunity to travel with them for several weeks.

I soon became frustrated on this trip, because I wasn't able to fulfill my desire to spend time alone with Shree Maa. There were fifteen of us traveling with her, and when she stopped in a city, many people wanted to see her. When she wasn't seeing people, she spent most of her time in seclusion.

One morning while I was meditating, I felt this desire to connect with her in a particularly intense way. My mind was telling me that I didn't need this personal contact because the Guru is within, but my heart was feeling a deep longing. I asked my inner voice to give me some direction. My inner voice said, "The desire you have to get close to Shree Maa is a good one. Go with that feeling." I replied to my inner voice, "What should I do, then?" My inner voice said, "Pray to Ramakrishna."

At that point, I knew that Ramakrishna and Shree Maa were intimately connected, so I prayed to Ramakrishna and pleaded, "Please, let me get close to Shree Maa." Then my inner voice said, "Good. Now open your eyes." When I opened my eyes, I saw Shree Maa coming down the steps of the house. She walked directly up to me and asked, "Would you like to take a walk with me?"

That walk was a turning point in my relationship with Shree Maa and ushered in a new level of intimacy with her.

· BOOK TWO ·
CONVERSATIONS WITH
SWAMI SATYANANDA

6

INTRODUCTION TO SWAMI SATYANANDA

Swami Satyananda's story is no less amazing than Shree Maa's. After completing his university education in the United States, Swami decided to see some of the world before he went to work full-time in the corporate culture. However, God had other plans for him. When he arrived in India, he was so intoxicated by its spiritual essence that he couldn't leave. He ended up spending the next twenty years of his life there.

After arriving in India, he quickly headed for the Himalayas, feeling he would find what he wanted there. His search led him to the feet of his Guru, who taught him much of his wisdom and eventually ordained him as a Swami.

After his Guru left his body, Swami traveled around India, stopping to meditate at temples and holy places. It was in one of these small temples that Shree Maa appeared to him and began a relationship that still continues today.

In 1984, after spending several years together in India, Shree Maa and Swami came to the United States to bring their wisdom to the West. Their early years in the U.S. were spent in semi-retreat. During that time Swami performed intensive spiritual practices and translated many of the ancient scriptures of India to make them more accessible to Westerners. During the last few years, Swami and Shree Maa have been traveling around the world, offering free programs of devotional singing and instruction.

Swami's playfulness is one of the qualities I love most about him. He has a unique ability to combine heartfelt reverence with a tongue-in-cheek irreverence. He is funny, spontaneous and constantly joking and playing. Swami is the rare holy man who doesn't take himself too seriously.

Swami is also a fireball of energy who is in constant service to humanity. His dedication is so great that he stops only occasionally for a little sleep, yet he always has time for someone in need. If you went into his office, which is a small trailer that can barely hold three people, you would see four computers and three printers arrayed in front of him. It's so incongruous to see this man, who used to live alone in the most primitive conditions, knee-deep in modern technology, bringing the ancient teachings of India to the West.

While we often think of holy men as ethereal, Swami is extremely down to earth and competent. As a former tank commander, he's used to getting his hands on things. In the early years of the ashram, he was its hardest worker, driving a bulldozer and wielding a sledgehammer and chain saw.

It's unparalleled to find a Westerner who has spent so much time in India as a Swami and has returned to live in the West once again. Fortunately, he has the skill to communicate the wisdom of India in a frank, straightforward manner that makes it understandable to Westerners. Instead of talking about dry theory, Swami speaks from his own personal experience.

In these interviews, Swami breathes life into the wisdom of India and shows us how we can apply these teachings to our daily lives.

7
Travels In India

Falling In Love

Why did you stay in India instead of continuing your travels around the world?

I fell in love. I just loved it there so much. There is a space of mind in India where people have time and consideration and concern and devotion. All these terms are not just words. In India they are living experiences.

Did you feel that right away?

I felt it right away. I met some Indian people when I was riding in the bus from Pakistan to Amritsar, India. They asked me, "Where will you stay when you get to Amritsar?" I answered, "Do you know of any hostel or cheap hotel?" They said, "When you get to Amritsar, there is only one place to stay, the Golden Temple." I had been through many countries on my trip so far, and no one had said, "Go stay in the temple."

And that's one of the fanciest and most famous temples in India, right?

That's right. So I got to the temple, and here I was, this disheveled young foreigner. I went up to the man who seemed to be in charge and said, "I would like to stay somewhere. Can you recommend a place for me?" The man said, "Here's the key to a room down at the end of the hall. There's a place for a bath right around the corner. Go to the temple, and they will feed you and give you everything else you may need." I asked, "How much money do you charge?" He replied, "There's no charge. This is a temple."

This whole thing absolutely intrigued me. I had been greeted in many cities and many countries, and nobody had said, "Come stay in the temple and eat all you want and enjoy your stay, and we won't charge you anything." So I asked him, "How can you offer this kind of hospitality?" and he said, "Those who can give, give to the temple, and those who can't give, don't give. This is God's house. Everyone is a child of God, so everyone is qualified to stay here. Why shouldn't you receive God's hospitality?"

Then I went to my room, and it was a very nice room. So I took a bath and I walked around and saw the devotion and sincerity of the people. The Golden Temple was very beautiful, and people were singing and playing music, and I got drawn into learning about what was happening. That began my sojourn in the temples of India.

After that I wandered from temple to temple and I learned more of the language and the customs and traditions. I learned that it was my right to stay in the temples. It wasn't so much that I was a guest anymore. I felt like I was a citizen of the world. I was a child of God. The temples are God's temples and a place for devotees to share and worship in love and joy. I had no thought of going back ever.

Going back to the United States?

Going back anywhere. Never going back. I never thought about going back and I haven't "gone back" since. I've only gone forward. I never had anything that I wanted to go back

to, that I loved more than being in love with God and being in love with life. What could be better than the respect and joy, appreciation and community, camaraderie and singing and dancing and the sharing of love that I was experiencing?

You see the way I work here. Well, I worked in India in a similar way. I wasn't sitting in front of a computer, but I studied diligently. I did projects for different communities. I did work for temples and ashrams. I chopped wood and carried water and made roads. I taught English and I taught philosophy. I shared knowledge of many subjects in many ways.

As I became more and more a resident of the temples, I taught spirituality and meditation and puja to Indian people who wanted to know more about their culture. Indian people are locked into one social economic environment. Wealthy people can't leave their environment to go hang out on a curb side with poor people. Poor people can't enter the house of a wealthy person. I was a foreigner, an explorer, a traveler, a businessman. So I was accepted everywhere. I had the latitude to see India in ways that Indians couldn't see their own country. I could hang out with the richest of the rich and the poorest of the poor. It was just fascinating!

Didn't you miss the comforts of home?

No. The joys of India were more than sufficient to compensate for the small sacrifices in comfort I gave up. The bouts I had with dysentery and malaria and filaria and hepatitis were just minor inconveniences. It was a small price to pay for the experience of openness I felt.

I was welcome everywhere! I could take a blanket and throw it over my shoulder and walk down the road. I had a begging bowl in my hand, a little bag with a diary and a couple of pens, one toothbrush, a dry loincloth and I was ready to go anywhere.

Is that all you had?

That's all I had.

Did you have any money?

I did at first, and then it was gone. Then I found ways to interact with India that didn't require money.

You didn't know where your next meal was coming from?

Many, many times I didn't know where my next meal was coming from, but I always knew that God would take care of me. I had no doubt about that whatsoever. I knew I could appear in any tea stall in any village, sing a song and tell a story and, in no time at all, I would have a cup of tea and biscuits, an invitation for dinner and usually a nice, warm, dry place to sleep.

What happened when you didn't get that?

I sat under a tree in the rain.

And that didn't bother you?

No. I was wet and I was cold, but I was singing. What an experience! Every atom of the sky was singing with me.

Really?

Yes. All the trees in the forest were chanting mantras with me. Every star in the sky was shining on me. There were many, many nights I slept outside. It was so exciting.

You were so happy and fulfilled that nothing bothered you?

Yes. You can see by my life today. It's so exciting. You can put me on top of a mountain with nothing at all, and I can find the excitement.

Traveling With The Guru

So you were traveling around for a while and then you met a Guru?

I met many Gurus and then I met a particular Guru with whom I studied and traveled and went deeper into the customs, languages and systems of worship. Then he sent me out to other Gurus. He said, "No one individual has all the answers. Not even me. I can tell you a lot about my subjects, but you're going to want to know many subjects in order to be a well-rounded sadhu. So learn some things from me, and I'll help coordinate your various experiences. I'm sending you to one place to learn asanas (hatha yoga postures) and to another place to learn pranayama (yogic breathing) and to still another place to learn history." He sent me to many teachers. After three months or six months or a year, I came back to our center and said, "This is what I learned!" He said, "Great! This is very good, and this is not of so much value. Now, how are you going to integrate these teachings into your life?"

What was your daily life like with him?

Well, we had two life-styles: in the ashram and outside the ashram. Outside the ashram was a very exciting period of my life. Just the two of us traveled together. We had a vow that for three years we wouldn't sit under a roof. That meant that every night we would sleep outside under the stars. During the rainy season, we would sleep on the veranda of a temple.

We would arrive at a campsite and first find where the water and wood were, and that would determine where we would stay. After gathering our wood, we would brush away the debris and make a level place, put some leaves down and put a small blanket on the leaves. Then we would take a shower in a creek or a river. We bathed four or five times a day. That's very important to our tradition. Every time we took a bath, we would wash at least our undergarments, if not everything. We carried three sets of clothes with us. One set was always clean and folded. Another set we would wear, and another would be on the line drying.

Then we would sit down. If it was late afternoon, we would make a fire and have some tea. Then we would chant for an hour or so and meditate for two hours. Around seven o'clock, we would make a light meal. Usually we would have chapatis (small Indian breads). We would slap the chapatis, because we didn't have a roller. We would make the chapatis right on the coals. We would also have some dahl. In the dahl we would put potato or whatever was available. In the beds of the creeks of the Himalayas, we would find lingra, which are ferns that grow on the side of the creek

94

that taste like asparagus. You could find chimara, which are little apple berries that you'd find on the trees. We had a jar of masala and one of salt, and we'd put some salt and masala in the dahl. We'd carry one or two vessels for cooking.

Then we'd clean up and wash the dishes and sit around the fire and talk into the night. Or he'd sing a hymn or translate a song. He used to go into very beautiful spaces to translate a song.

In the morning, we would usually get up around 4:00 or 4:30 AM. It would be dark outside. We would put some kindling on the fire and make it burn again. When the fire was going, we would take our bath, no matter how cold the river was. After bathing, we would warm up by the fire. We never made warm water for bathing. We used to always bathe in cold water. Then, when we got warm and toasty, we would sit under our blankets and meditate. When dawn broke, we would make a cup of tea. Then we would do puja.

Some places we stayed for three days, other places we just stayed for a little while and then moved on. If we stayed somewhere, then after puja we would spend most of the day chanting. We would make one meal during the middle of the day or in the evening, or sometimes two meals a day if it felt right. Otherwise, we would have some biscuits and a cup of tea.

Weren't you hungry?

No. My body weight reduced significantly. I was in my prime. I felt really good and energetic. I didn't need much food or sleep. I was feeling very sattvic (pure) and very clean. I had a lot more energy.

On the days we would move, we would break camp around 9:00 AM, clean up the campsite, take what we needed and walk off down the path. You will find a temple every two or three miles along the mountain trails. We would stop at every temple and sit and rest, make friends and tell stories and have a cup of tea. When we reached a little village, people would invite us to come in. They invited us constantly.

Did you travel this way for months?

For years. We went for three years like that. Then he went to West Bengal, and I went to meet another Guru in a different place. Among other subjects, I studied hatha yoga and asanas. One time I came back to our room in an ashram in Vrindaban, and there was a note on the bed that said, "I am in a little village in West Bengal. If you want to come see me, you are welcome." So I got on a train, then a bus, then took a rickshaw to the end of the road. Then I got on a bullock cart and went as far as it would go. Then I walked for two days into the interior of West Bengal. I swam across a couple of rivers, because there weren't any bridges. Finally, I came to a little island in the middle of a river I still don't know the name of. It was an extremely remote area with ancient, dilapidated temples for the Divine Mother. My Guru was there with another sadhu, and we stayed there for some days.

One day my Guru told me to demonstrate my hatha yoga postures in front of the other Guru and his disciples. I was quite nervous, as I had never "performed" with other people looking, but I gathered courage and quite proficiently executed my routine. The other Guru was extremely impressed and said to his disciples, "See, foreigners come from such a distance to learn our culture, and what are we practicing? We ourselves don't know our own dharma."

My Guru said to me, "That was excellent. Now you don't have to practice hatha yoga anymore."

I was stunned. "Why not?" I asked.

"Because the purpose of practicing hatha yoga is to be able to sit still for the more subtle forms of yoga," he replied sternly, "not to become a performer of stunts to impress others. That will only enhance the ego. Our sadhana is to be still in order to reduce the ego."

Meditating In The Cremation Grounds

We traveled to many different types of ashrams, and I performed many different kinds of sadhana. I spent a lot of time in cremation grounds. I felt a powerful sense of detachment and renunciation sitting by the burning pyres. I felt that nothing had the power to bind me. I would contemplate what was really important in my life. The more I sat in the cremation grounds, the more I got comfortable with those emotions. I learned the process of burning the bodies. I met many sadhus there. Some of it was very freaky and far out, and some of it was right on and very beautiful.

I liked to chant the *Chandi* by the light of the funeral pyre, because it burns very brightly and you can easily read at night.

Did you feel afraid at the cremation grounds?

No. I felt very much at home, very peaceful. When I first started coming to the cremation grounds, it was a little frightening, because it was at night, and there was darkness and death, and the villagers would talk about ghosts and goblins. But once you've been in the cremation grounds for a while, you realize that the worst that can happen is death. Once you've confronted death and you're not clinging to the attachments of life, what could happen to you? What do you have to lose?

I heard that you became so absorbed in God while at the cremation grounds that sometimes you would wake up in somebody else's house. Is that true?

Yes. I would go into samadhi on many occasions, because I was doing a strong discipline. I would sit in one asana

(cross-legged sitting posture) for ten or twelve hours at a
time without breaking the posture. So when I went into
meditation in the nighttime, there were many times when I
lost consciousness of my body completely. It is customary
that when the burning of the body is completed, people
would put out the fire with buckets of water and then sweep
the area clean. They would throw the debris into the river. If
I was sitting by the fire in samadhi, they didn't want to
offend me by throwing a bucket of water and having the
water splash on me. So there were times when they picked
me up and carried me away. When I woke up, I would find

myself in another location and still locked in my sitting posture.

Were you aware of them picking you up and carrying you?

No. There were many times when I woke up in a temple or in somebody's house. They didn't want to stay there all day watching me meditate and they had to clean up the site before they left, so they carried me away with them.

There was a period of my life when I went in and out of samadhi a lot, especially in the cremation grounds of Bakreshwar.

What is the appeal of samadhi if you aren't even there? Or are you there?

There is an experience, but the experience that can be talked about isn't samadhi. You can talk about going into samadhi and you can talk about coming out of samadhi.

But are you having an experience even though you can't put words to it?

In a sense that is true. But there is no "me" to be having the experience. Another way to describe the experience that I have had personally is that everything is an extension of me. Every atom of creation is me. So I am having an experience of being all of existence. My "I" expanded; it didn't disappear. It expanded into the totality of existence.

Is this experience extremely pleasurable?

It is belittling the experience of bliss to talk about it in terms of pleasure.

Is it so wonderful, for lack of a better word, that you want to keep reexperiencing it?

Not necessarily. It is so wonderful that you want to serve God in any way She chooses. That could be by not going into samadhi as a conscious sacrifice for God. I know how to go into samadhi, but I love God so much that I'm willing to sacrifice what people would consider to be the most wonderful spiritual experience in order to serve Her in any way I can.

Would that kind of unselfish love be a consequence of going into samadhi?

I believe the more you experience Her and the more you love Her, the more you accept that samadhi isn't the greatest thing in the world. She is. If She allows you to go into samadhi, when you come out you want to serve Her in any way you can.

The Howrah Train Station

Okay, so back to the story. What happened next?

At one point we came down from the Himalayas and went to Calcutta and arrived in the Howrah train station. We got off the train and my Guru said, "It's early morning, and we've just arrived. Let's take a shower and sit down right here and read the *Chandi*."

I said, "Guruji, I think that's absurd! Why don't we go someplace that is more peaceful?" He said, "Anyone can meditate in the Himalayas. Now you are going to have to learn to live in the world and maintain that same attitude of peace."

And this train station is huge, right? There are thousands of people there.

Right.

And you were sitting down on the platform where everybody was walking back and forth?

Yes.

What was that like?

At first I thought it was ridiculous. The coolies were spitting at us, and everyone was pushing us. People were shouting, "Hey, what are you doing? Move out of the way!" There was always somebody pushing at me, pulling at me, poking at me. The objective was to maintain my asana and not miss a breath or mispronounce a word of the *Chandi*. That meant giving no response to anybody whatsoever. I had to be so absorbed in the *Chandi*, so disciplined, that I could ignore anything that was going on around me for five or six hours at a time.

How long did it take to be able to do that?

A couple of weeks.

Wow! That's amazing. Were you in bhava samadhi (a samadhi where you retain awareness of your separate self)?

Yes, it was a bhava samadhi. You get into such a state of absorption that the only reality is the *Chandi*. The maya of people pushing and shoving and yelling and poking is all part of the dream. The reality is *Chandi*, which is the stage of consciousness, and all of the maya is the drama that is presented upon the stage. Reading the *Chandi* trains you to do this.

Everything but the Chandi *is background noise.*

Yes. It's all background noise, and I'm paying attention to the foreground noise. Right now you and I are having this conversation while the river is flowing. We are hearing the river in the background, but we're also hearing the words that are being spoken. In the same way, the *Chandi* is in the foreground, and all the other noise of existence is in the background.

So if you are sitting with God, what else is important? I love that!

Yes.

Traveling Alone

What happened after your Guru left his body?

When he left his body, I was filled with grief. I kept thinking, "What will I do?" I was feeling bereft, as though I had lost my goal. Then a voice came from within that said, "I'm inside you. You are no longer dependent on the Guru. The Guru is within. You are the Guru."

So I went off to do sadhana. I went to many places. I crossed Northern India. I stayed in the wilds and the jungles, especially in the mountains between Bengal and Bihar. This is where many tribal people live, the Santal Parganas, a five-day walk from the nearest bazaar. I would find a lonely place and sit down and chant the *Chandi* every day. Whenever possible, I performed fire ceremonies.

In this way, I wandered into Rishikesh. I wanted to perform a yajna (fire ceremony) there, but didn't have a place. One sannyasini (female monk) took me to a man who owned a broken-down house on the bank of the Ganges. It had a wall around it and a little Shiva temple inside the courtyard. It was totally neglected and abandoned. He said I could stay there as long as I liked. So I cleaned up the house and repaired it. They started to bring me food occasionally. When I got it all fixed up, I sat down and performed a three-year Sahasra Chandi, three years of reciting the *Chandi Path* before the sacred fire without leaving the temple grounds. It was during that time that I translated the *Chandi Path* into English.

What was your schedule like there?

All year around, I got up at four o'clock in the morning and took a bath in the Ganges. After bathing, I would make myself tea. I would only make a quarter of a cup in the morning and a quarter of a cup in the evening. I was sitting for long hours in one asana (posture). One of the greatest difficulties I had was controlling the urge to urinate. I didn't want to get up and break my asana. So I reduced my water intake significantly in order to control that urge. I figured since the water has to come out, I just have to restrict how much goes in. Therefore, I only took a half cup in the morning and a half cup in the evening.

I would sit in one posture from morning until night. Sometimes I would vary the program according to the days of the lunar fortnight. From the first day until the fifth day, I would do the Cosmic Puja. Then I'd get up and take a half-hour break. Then I'd sit down and sing the *Chandi* as many as five times in the same asana, which would take seven and a half to eight hours a day. From the sixth day until the full or new moon, I wouldn't take that half-hour break.

Why would you choose to chant the Chandi *instead of just being in samadhi?*

Well, the *Chandi* puts you into a bhava samadhi, the attitude of oneness. The mantras are written in a certain meter that requires you to breathe according to this meter. When you watch the drama of the *Chandi*, you watch the demise of Too Much and Too Little, the surrender of Self-Conceit and Self-Deprecation, the eradication of the Great Ego. You watch this drama on the stage of consciousness. You watch it going on inside. All your old memories go into the fire. All your past history is consumed.

Then you get to the end of the *Chandi*, to the thirteenth chapter, where the businessman who lost his business and the king who lost his kingdom chant the *Chandi*. At that point, the Goddess comes to them and says, "I am very pleased by the devotion you are showing. What do you want?" The king answers, "I want my kingdom back." The Divine Mother replies, "I give you that boon. You are the King of Good Thoughts, and no evil thought can ever enter into your kingdom." Then she asks the businessman what he wants, and he answers, "Mother, I am so pleased that you are blessing me with a gift like the *Chandi*. I don't want anything else. I just want the privilege of surrendering to you. Give me the highest wisdom and the bliss of freedom from attachment." She says, "Tathastu. I give you the boon. You will remain in the highest wisdom, and your name will be Samadhi. Your karma and your name are one; you will always be in samadhi. Whether sitting or standing or

walking or talking, you are Samadhi. That is your true identity."

Then that's no longer a state that you go into; it's a state that you stay in all the time. You are Samadhi. So when She says that to you every day for three years, after a while you begin to listen to Her, because you know what it means. Your only commitment from day until night is to chant the *Chandi*.

So you were always in bhava samadhi? You were in bliss all the time?

Yes, yes. During that period of time, I also translated the *Chandi*. So after I finished chanting the *Chandi*, I would prepare some food. I had one meal in the evening. Then I would work on the translation.

I saw nobody, except for a man who brought me groceries once a week. I had no phone, no TV, no radio, no newspaper, no magazine. I didn't talk to anybody. I had only the *Chandi*, some scriptures and some books on philosophy. That was my life for three years in Rishikesh. I loved it!

I performed the Sahasra Chandi four times. The Sahasra Chandi takes three years to complete, and you don't leave the temple during that time. I performed it once in Rishikesh, once in Bhageshwar, once in Bakreshwar and once in Martinez, California. During those periods of time, my only occupation was the Goddess.

After that first Sahasra Chandi was completed, I got up from my asana and asked, "Okay, Mother, how do You want me to serve You?"

Then I traveled and met other Gurus and saints and I sat in every temple and sang the *Chandi*. I had a wonderful time. People were so respectful and appreciative. They thought, "Our ancient culture is so appealing that someone from the United States has left everything and come here to devote his life to the *Chandi*."

Did they have resistance to you being a Westerner?

Many people did. In many temples I met with resistance. But in most places, when they saw my sincerity and knowledge, they were friendly.

Were you doing these retreats before you met Shree Maa?

Yes. I used to lock myself in any temple that felt conducive. I would arrange a supply line for myself that would provide all the necessary provisions for the sustenance of the body as well as the materials that are necessary for doing pujas. Once I created the supply line, I would lock myself in the temple for nine, thirty or one hundred and eight days, sometimes even three years.

Literally lock yourself in?

Yes. I did this in many temples around India. I would find a temple that had a door on it that I could lock from the inside.

They were small temples?

Yes. Basically one room. I would sit in the temple and perform my pujas and meditations. That's the way almost fifteen years went by.

What was the appeal of sitting inside one room all day long?

It was absolutely blissful! I had no desire to go outside, because I had everything I wanted. I was completely content and filled with delight.

Meeting Shree Maa

Could you tell us about the experience of meeting Shree Maa?

Certainly. I was doing a 108-day retreat in a small temple in Bakreshwar. Pachu was a young man of the village who would provide the preparations for my puja. Then he would close the gate and lock it with a padlock on the outside. He would then throw the key in through the window in order to ensure that no one could disturb me.

After sixty days had passed, I thought that I might go to the Kamakhya Temple to make my next vow of worship. About this time, Shree Maa was meditating in the Kamakhya Temple and got the message to go to Bakreshwar to see me.

It was a few weeks later when one morning Pachu came into the temple and said to me, "One Mataji is here looking for you. She wants to take darshan in this temple."

I said, "Pachu, I haven't seen anyone in more than two months. We have only a few weeks to go. Please don't bring anybody into the temple now."

He said, "She is a really radiant and pure soul. She just wants to look at the temple and see the place where you are worshiping, and then she will go."

"I'm not interested," I replied. "I don't want to be late for my worship. If I start late, I won't finish until late, and as you know, then I have to light the hurricane lantern to see the last mantras, and my nose gets black from breathing the kerosene fumes."

I went into my room and saw through the crack in the door that several people were walking into our little temple. They all sat down like sardines in a can and began meditating.

I called Pachu and complained, "What are all of these people doing meditating in the temple? How did they come in? Get them out! I have to begin my worship!"

Pachu said, "I can't send them out. I can't tell them they can't meditate in a temple! That's why we make temples!"

I got up and went outside the door of the temple and started pacing back and forth. I started to cough and clear my throat. I tried to make as much of a disturbance as I possibly could. Nobody moved. It had been forty-five minutes already, and I was getting angry.

Finally a man came out. He looked at me and his eyes lit up. "Oh, you are a foreigner! Have you seen the Taj Mahal?" He started to question me about all the sights of India.

I blew my cool. In the nicest village slang I knew, I said, "You are the foreigner. This is my temple. You people are disturbing my meditation. Pick yourselves up and go sit in somebody else's temple. I've got work to do! Don't come talking to me about the Taj Mahal and making me late for my worship!"

Hearing the commotion, all of the people came out from the temple. They were all city people, wearing pants and shirts, respectable, city-type clothes, not like the dress of the people of our village.

As if on cue, the people parted, and Shree Maa came out from the temple and walked up the aisle between the devotees. Her face was more radiant than anything I could have imagined. She had been crying, and tears were rolling down her cheeks. She was so luminous, so majestic. She walked straight toward me.

She looked me in the eye, and I knew her immediately. In the eyes of Shree Maa, I saw the exact image of Kali, the deity that I had been worshiping for years. Her eyes shined in the same way. She had tears running down the sides of her face. She was incandescent. So much truth and purity radiated from her face. I was astonished that the Goddess would come to me. I never even considered it to be a possibility. I always saw her without form or as the form of all existence. I never thought that an individual could reflect in her entirety, the purity, clarity and determination of the Divine Mother. I knew it at first sight. I didn't know who she was, where she came from, what her name was or anything else about her.

My jaw fell open in astonishment, and so gracefully, without the least hesitation, she reached up and put a sweet into my mouth and just looked at me. We stared into each other's eyes for what must have been an eternity. Then she put a flower on my head, turned around and walked between the two rows of people. Without looking back, she walked right out through the gate. Then all the people turned and followed her out. No one spoke a word. Then I was alone with a flower on my head and a sweet in my mouth.

I stood there, staring in disbelief. She was the Goddess I had been worshiping, and I had made such a fuss about being late for worship. It was She whom I had been calling. Who was She?

I couldn't follow her, because I had taken a vow to complete my worship, and nothing can break that vow. I went into the temple and looked into Kali's face. It was the exact image of

Shree Maa. I performed the worship, but all I could see was Shree Maa's face.

"Who was she? Where was she from?" All these questions continually came to my mind, but nobody could find out anything about her. All anybody knew was that a group of tourists had spent a few hours in the temples of the area and left.

Can you say more about what you mean when you said that Shree Maa was the same as the deity you had been worshiping?

I had two photographs that I carried around with me. One was of the Goddess Chandi, the same picture on the cover of my translation of the *Chandi Path* book. I made some copies of that picture and established them in every temple I went to. I also had a picture of the Goddess Kali. This Kali had a blue face and was very benign.

When I saw Shree Maa, I saw those images. She had the same type of eyes and the same type of smile, the same glow. So between the two images of the Goddess I had been worshiping, Shree Maa was the exact image of both of them.

That must have been quite an experience!

It was an amazing experience, because I saw her after I had just gotten through throwing all these people out of the ashram. That made it all the more astounding, because I had just been very rude and told everybody to get out.

What a time to meet Shree Maa (laughing)!

Yes (laughing). That was the last thing I expected to see in that moment when I was extremely anxious because I was late for worship and didn't want to be bothered by all those people. It was a great teaching, because now when someone wants something from me and I feel imposed upon, I try to remember to see that person as God knocking on my door.

Can you say more about how you next came to see Shree Maa?

After I completed my vow, she immediately led me to her. I was on my way to another temple and I found myself within a few days on Shree Maa's doorstep.

Once I got to the house she was staying at, it turned out that she had been expecting me. From that point on, it was just amazing. She saw me and said, "We'll do puja now." They led me to the puja room, and everything was set up. There were big baskets of flowers and large copper and brass utensils. Everything was shining, and all the food was cooked. It was all set up for me like I never had it set up before. I had been a village pujari (priest) worshiping behind closed doors with little bells and little platters and little paper plates.

It was a nice-sized living room in someone's house, and I was ready to take a seat in the back of the room. She said, "No, you sit up here." They sat me down, and I was very nervous because I had never done puja in front of people before. All these years I was doing puja alone, and now there were fifty people sitting there.

So I turned to Shree Maa and said, "Mother, I've never done puja in front of people before." She said, "Forget about the people. You're doing puja in front of God."

After the puja, we went outside, and there were a few hundred people, and we performed a yajna and it got to be really fun. It was exciting. Then she put me on a stage in a school playground and told me to give a talk in Hindi.

(Laughing) I said, "You're going a little too far!"

She put you in that position right away.

Yes. I had no preparation, no training. I had no concept I would be singing and praying and telling stories all over the world.

You went from being completely isolated and not seeing anybody to being surrounded by people all the time.

Yes. I had no idea that this was going to occur. My predisposition was toward solitude.

Traveling With Shree Maa

How long did you and Shree Maa travel around India together?

We met in the beginning of 1980 and we traveled to the U.S. in late 1984. It was about five years. We traveled around India producing festivals of worship. We went into a village and prepared deities ourselves. People would raise a circus tent over our heads. We would get wood and have big yajnas. Some of the crowds got very big.

Then Ramakrishna told Shree Maa to come to the U.S.?

Ramakrishna had already told Shree Maa to go to the United States and to travel around the world. She told me that sometime after we met, and I said, "I'm staying in India!"

You hadn't been back to the U.S. in fifteen years at that point?

Even more. Then in 1984, she said, "We have to go to foreign countries." As it turned out, we went to Bangladesh to perform a yajna and when we were going back to India, the Indian government wouldn't allow me back in. They said, "You've been in India long enough. You've used up every excuse you have. There is no way we can give you another visa according to our current laws." So we were stuck in Bangladesh. Then we came to the U.S. thinking that I could get a fresh passport and start all over again.

So you arrived in the U.S. with practically nothing?

Just what we took to Bangladesh, which was supposed to be a trip for a couple of weeks. All we had was a few books and changes of clothing.

When we came to America, I got a new passport, and the Indian consulate said that no new visas were being given out at that time. It turns out that my citizenship in India had been granted, but they didn't know where to find me.

We started doing some small programs in California, and we realized that all of our teaching materials were in Bengali and Sanskrit. We had nothing in English. Nobody could participate in our programs. So I started making transliterations of Sanskrit with a typewriter.

Shree Maa at first said it would be a greater teaching for people to see us go into samadhi. So she would be in samadhi, and I would sit there trying to do a ceremony, waiting for her to come back. She was in the habit of staying in samadhi for five hours at a time.

We gave a talk at a college, and I said, "Mother, I'll tell a story, we'll have a five-minute meditation, and you can sing a song." We meditated, and she went into samadhi. I kept waiting for her to sing her song. Then I went into samadhi. When we both woke up near the end of the day, there was a janitor sweeping the floor, and the room was empty. Everybody had left, except the janitor. People didn't understand what was happening. They got bored when they saw two people sitting on the floor, smiling, with their eyes closed.

So Shree Maa and I made a conscious decision not to go into samadhi.

Do you mean you decided to not go into samadhi just when giving a program or all the time?

Well, we started living with devotees, so there were people around all the time.

That was quite a sacrifice.

That's true. It was a significant sacrifice.

Is that still going on?

Well, we go into samadhi in private now, but we don't have much privacy. We are busy creating the learning tools for people to do sadhana. Now Mother gets some time, but I get very little.

I said to Shree Maa, "You know, it would be very easy for us to live in India for the rest of our lives and stay in samadhi. That would be very delightful and very comfortable and very joyous." And she said, "That's not our dharma. Our dharma is to teach and inspire people who are in the world."

Did you want to do that?

No. So I had the choice of leaving Mother and following my own path or following her. I was confident that Mother's path is the path of purity, so I surrendered to her. Often I think how I would love to leave this and go to India, but I made a decision to help her in her work.

Thank you.

You're welcome.

That must have been quite an adjustment, to not go into samadhi.

Yes. It was a big adjustment to go to a hall and have to be finished at a certain time. The first time we did a public puja in the U.S., we did it at an ashram, and the people there said, "How are you going to advertise your puja?" We said, "Why would we advertise?" They said, "Who is going to come?"

We said, "God. Who else would you want to come to a puja?"

We are trying to propagate the dharma by preparing teaching tools. We don't want to proselytize or start enrolling people and create an organization. We just want to share the dharma and inspire people to make their relationship with God vibrant.

Overview

8

WHY ALL THIS INDIAN STUFF?

Swami, why should a Westerner follow a spiritual path that originates from the East? Doesn't it make more sense to create our own spiritual systems that are congruent with the culture we live in?

All known religions come from the East, including Christianity, Buddhism and Hinduism. The forms of worship that we are using that have emanated from the East are traditions that have worked for people who attained the goal. We are studying and practicing them because they are systems that have worked. They put the body, mind and consciousness into harmony and allow absorption into total divinity. Therefore, we are not trying to create a new system. Why reinvent the wheel? If it works, use it.

Westerners can be put off by the Indian forms of spirituality. For instance, depictions of Gods and Goddesses can seem strange and garish. How can one get past that reaction?

According to our philosophy, there is one divinity that manifests itself in every atom of existence. That means we can take any object of creation and call that "my" form of divinity. We perceive divinity in that form, and that will be the object that we revere.

If you have a difficulty with the forms of Indian Gods and Goddesses, then you can use a candle and worship it with the same system of worship. In the Vedic period, which was before all the deities came into their present forms, they worshiped the forms of nature. They saw in the river's rush of water the flow of life always seeking unity with the ocean, the infinite expanse. Water always takes the form of the container you put it into. Water is the perfect allegory for the flow and balance of life. They saw in the wind the qualities of God that are unchecked and unrestrained. No one can harness the wind. The patience of the wind can blow down mountains. So the wind is an allegory for perfect freedom.

So we can use anything as an object of worship?

Any form you choose. It's all God. So when you choose a form for worship, you are saying, "I know God is infinite beyond conception; however, I can't conceive of infinity beyond conception. I want something finite that I can see and think about."

Is it true that the rishis (holy men) would worship a rock, and that was the origination of the Shiva lingam?

Yes, but that's only a portion of it. In the Vedic era, the rishis wandered from place to place and never stayed anywhere more than three days, because they didn't want to cultivate attachment. They would sit underneath a tree and perform their spiritual practices. People would come to the tree and they would say to the rishi, "Revered soul, when you are sitting with us, we have no trouble understanding what you teach. You convey so much inspiration that our lives are transformed. However, when you go away, we forget. The delusion of our attachments is so strong that we can't maintain the same perception when you are away. What can we do to maintain this attitude of devotion?"

The rishi said, "You see this stone. This is an emblem of divinity. This is the lingam of Shiva, the symbol of infinite goodness. Come here every day and worship this lingam. Give it a glass of water and give it a flower and remember all the wisdom and joy we shared when we were together. Think what a joy it is to be in the presence of a symbol of divinity. That is a way to remember." This was how the first forms of worship began.

In this example, people are remembering a communion with a great soul. What if you haven't met such a person and you are sitting with the symbol without that memory?

Books are filled with the wisdom of those great souls. Read the scriptures and commune with their wisdom. In olden times, they wrote down the words of the rishis and they passed them with great reverence from generation to generation, from Guru to disciple. If you don't have the physical presence of a person who inspires you, read a scripture. Sit by a symbol of divinity and listen to the wisdom of the wise.

If you read the words from the wise and you are sitting in front of a symbol of divinity, will a presence manifest itself?

Before you sow a seed, you have to plow the field. So the first thing that happens is you have to commune with wisdom more than you do with your material attachments. As that desire grows greater and greater, your motivation, focus and inspiration become stronger. Ultimately, the Guru will manifest.

So the Guru will come?

Yes, without a doubt. He or She will come in some form. Many of us say, "God, please come and visit me," and when we look around we see that our house is a mess. And we say, "Please come, God, and help me with my problems." But very few people are willing to gather flowers, light the incense and prepare food because God is coming.

Do you have to believe that God is going to come?

Certainly. If I invite you to dinner, don't I believe you are going to come?

126

But you are saying you have to believe first. What if you don't? What if you haven't had the experience and you aren't sure such a thing could occur?

Faith is cultivated through practice. We are saying, "Even though there may be some doubt about the validity of all these practices, try them anyway and see. Try to put yourself into the same attitude that the people of old were in when they practiced these systems."

How do you get to the level of faith that makes you want to try the practices?

The only way to get that level of faith is through satsangha, communion with people who have it. You have to meet somebody who has the faith and then you will get enough faith to try it.

You see it works for them and then you think it may work for you?

Yes.

Do you have to believe in God to embark on this path?

What are we calling God? Are we looking for some being in the sky? Are we looking for the God in the Cecil B. Demille movies, where the clouds part and the voice of God thunders, or are we looking for the divinity that dwells in every atom of existence?

What if you're not sure if there is a higher power or something other than what you see?

If you are not sure there is a higher power or something other than what is empirically verifiable, then you are doubting your own existence. Obviously there is a power that is making me exist. There is a consciousness which allows me to function. It is the same consciousness that allows everybody else to function. I don't doubt that I function. How can I doubt that there is a higher power? It's a logical fallacy. So we are grabbing at straws and looking for excuses to justify our inaction. But that is not reality. Once you know that God is real, you have no other excuse but to get to work. Many of us want to excuse our laziness, so we say, "I doubt if there is a higher power. I doubt there is God."

Do you think there is a fear to get to work, and what would that fear be?

Yes, there is a fear. We think, "My life is very familiar to me. All of my value systems, all of my attachments, all of my prized possessions, the direction of my life: these are known and comfortable to me. Even though I may not be satisfied, it's familiar territory. Now you want to take me into realms I have never experienced before. Who knows what will happen? Who knows how my life might change?

"It's uncomfortable to sit, it's uncomfortable to look at my thoughts, it's uncomfortable to sort through my memories, it's uncomfortable to relive all my experiences. It's much better to busy myself with some worldly task and forget about the whole thing. It's much easier.

"Also, I have a fear of doing a foreign practice. Are you trying to make a fool of me? Are you trying to make me a servant to you? Are you trying to exercise your authority over me? What am I going to have to give up?"

There are so many doubts that creep in. In the *Chandi* one of the generals in the army of the Great Ego is named Devoid of Clear Understanding. He fills us with doubt. The more we doubt, the more it's impossible to perform effectively and take control of our lives. We become servants of the ego.

When we are doubting, we often aren't aware that we are doubting. The doubting thoughts seem very reasonable to us. What do you do when you are in that state of doubt?

"Where there is doubt, have faith." Those are the words of St. Francis.

How do you have that kind of faith?

The words of all of the people who were called wise beings were passed down from generation to generation. You have to have some faith in the authority of these words, these scriptures. That is why they have been passed down from generation to generation with such great care. You have to have some faith in the authority of wise beings who

129

live today. There must be somebody who is a being of wisdom. You can't discount all of the people of the world who believe in God just because you have your own doubt. So you have to cultivate faith. You have to argue with yourself, listening to the other side of the proposition that you are so vehemently challenging because of your doubts.

So it always begins with faith. You have to be willing to believe in something outside of your own thoughts.

When we took our first step as children, our parents said, "Come on! You can do it!" and we believed them. They encouraged us and inspired us, and we had faith and we stood up and we took that first step. That is what it takes every time, that kind of faith.

Why would one want to follow this path? What are the benefits?

We are cultivating holistic spirituality. We are not just learning about practices. We are learning about life. What you get out of it is a holistic life in which you can pay attention to everything you do and thereby realize the ultimate efficiency. You can fall in love with every being you meet, because once you know how to fall in love, you can turn it on any time you want to. You can perform every action with the same intensity. You can control your destiny. You can define your goals and find the path to their attainment. Instead of fitting into someone else's plan for your life, you create your own plan. You fill your heart with love and thereby eliminate loneliness.

Is that the goal of the path, love?

I would suggest the analogy of a pyramid. When you rise to the top, love, respect, attention, meditation are all one. They are all right up there at the top. At the base of the pyramid, there are separate emotions and feelings. When we are in our daily life, various activities manifest a portion of the feeling at the top of the pyramid. As we rise higher, we lose the selfish aspects of these feelings, which preclude the universality of that emotion. When we get to the top, they are all one. So the objective is love, joy, wisdom, peace and respect.

Is there a summit one reaches? Is there an end to the process?

There is really no end to loving. I remember when Jonathan Livingston Seagull rose to heaven and said, "This isn't the end of it at all. This is just the beginning!" There is just more and more love.

What are the dangers on this path?

The greatest danger is living without God. The greatest danger is taking whatever spiritual knowledge we attain and making it an appendage to the ego and walking around proclaiming our own greatness. In the sanatana dharma, the eternal ideal of perfection, we teach how to live with God in every moment.

131

9

Enlightenment And Chocolate Ice Cream

What is the fastest way to enlightenment?

As soon as we talk about speed in getting to a destination, we are defining the destination as an attainment. Enlightenment is not an attainment. It isn't something tangible that you can possess. Enlightenment is a realization in the moment. So the fastest way to enlightenment that I can suggest is to fall in love to the exclusion of all delusion. To fall in love — right now — with such force and conviction that you surrender all duality and all attachments to your beloved. Make that love the supreme love of all your loves.

What do you fall in love with?

Choose whatever you want. It could be chocolate ice cream, it could be a beautiful spouse, it could be your Guru, it could be God. Define it any way you want to.

So falling in love with chocolate ice cream could be the fastest way for me to become enlightened?

If your love of chocolate ice cream was great enough, it could take you to a place where all your thoughts stop and all you can remember is your beloved chocolate ice cream. Then you can expand that smaller love to a greater love. However, you may soon realize you want to fall in love with something that doesn't melt.

But when people fall in love with their girlfriend or their sports car, it doesn't usually lead them to a greater love.

There are two kinds of love. There's the love of selfish attachment, and there's the love of surrender. When we love selfishly, we only think about what's in it for me: I love you as long as my needs are fulfilled. When we love with unselfish surrender, we abandon all of our own personal considerations and give ourselves over to our beloved.

We're talking about falling in love with divine abandon, falling in love without any selfish motivation, without any ulterior motive. You can become in love with a clay statue or the wisdom of a book or the Guru who manifests the Grace of God or the infinite beyond conception. It's the same love affair.

Isn't it better to choose a divine object to love?

Divinity resides in every object of creation. Therefore, we can choose any object and say this is the divine. As we practice being a lover instead of sitting on the fence and waiting to be loved, we realize that we can project our love onto any object or being we choose.

What if you don't feel love. How do you get started?

Allow yourself to imagine what it would feel like if you were in love. You don't have to be in love. Just put yourself in the attitude of what it would be like if you were a saint and loved everyone. What does it look like, what does it feel like, what does it taste like, what thoughts am I thinking? It's play-acting. It's acting "as if" you were in love.

Many people may object and say, "I don't want to be phony." I would reply that this is a meditation. Pretend you are the greatest saint to walk the earth. Why not? It's your meditation. What is the purpose of our meditations? To fill ourselves with Godliness, to fill ourselves with the power of God, to empower ourselves with divinity.

It might help to think back to a time when you were in love and remember that feeling and apply it to the present. Then take that feeling and apply it to a flower or a candle.

Can you define enlightenment?

No. All the rishis in the Vedas said, "Neti, neti," it is not this and it is not that. So what can I say to define enlightenment? All I can suggest is that the consciousness of infinite goodness is approached by imagining the greatest goodness that you can conceive and making it better.

When you find that you can't imagine anything more wonderful, that's where you begin to define enlightenment.

Is it impossible to conceive it?

Of course it's impossible. It's a realization. So when we talk about the fastest way to get there, we are trying to make it a conception, an object of attainment. When we let go of the hope that we will attain enlightenment, then we can become enlightenment.

So the concept of enlightenment is just another attachment.

It's another attachment and it's an attempt to define in conceivable terms the inconceivable. So as long as we are striving for that conception, we are putting an obstacle in our own paths. When we let go of the concept, it is possible to fall in love so deeply that we pay full attention. When we pay attention to the exclusion of duality, and all that exists is the beloved, there is a state of enlightenment. When we come out of that state, we have the memory of what it's like to be in that state. We remember what it's like to feel full absorption, total commitment, no selfish attachment. From that memory, we act and interact in the world, and that's how the feeling of enlightenment permeates all our actions.

Would that absorption be called samadhi?

Yes. Samadhi is total absorption in the state of unity. It is the cessation of all duality. Samadhi is pure love, when we love so much that we cease to be.

135

When we come out of the samadhi, the memory of it remains in the background, while all the actions we perform in the world are in the foreground. So what do we want from the physical world? We want two things, the privilege to go back to that state of absorption and the joy of sharing the love that comes from that absorption. Then we dedicate our lives to those two propositions.

So you go in and out. Does sharing the love help you to go back in?

Definitely. You have to give it away to make it grow.

If you came out of samadhi and you didn't share the love, what would happen?

It would dissipate. The validity of any true spiritual experience is the change that it creates in our lives. Many people have reported marvelous visions and experiences while in meditation, but it's important to see what happened to their lives after that. Did they go back to the same personality and the same interactions, or did they start working for creation instead of working for themselves? Then we can see if it was a real experience.

Are there different kinds of samadhi?

Yes. There are three forms of samadhi. Bhava samadhi is the attitude of unity. In bhava samadhi there are three: I – love – you, the subject, the object and the relationship. Savikalpa samadhi means "with an idea." There are only two, I – you. The love is so intense that it is understood. You can't define it; you can only feel it. The love is so intense, you can't even express it as love, simply I am – you are. Nirvikalpa samadhi means "without an idea." It is just "You" or it's just "I."

Is there a witnessing aspect in savikalpa samadhi?

There is some awareness of separation. In nirvikalpa samadhi there is none.

If one experiences nirvikalpa samadhi, have they become enlightened?

No, they have not.

I know you have experienced samadhi many times. You have been in that state of perfection. Would you say it's a quantum leap in a sense? Would you say you're a normal person and then you jump into that state and then once you've experienced it, everything changes?

Well, certainly your values change. When you come out of that experience of perfection, it is not business as usual.

So you're a highly evolved but normal person and then you experience samadhi, and it's a whole new ball game?

When you come back from samadhi, you are still a normal person, but not completely. You know that God is a reality. You know that state of perfection is a reality. You know all the things that are in the books are true. Once you have

138

verified that for yourself, you will change. Your values will be different, your objectives will be different. You are no longer afforded the luxury of pretending it wasn't true. It demands you make a commitment, and life isn't the same once you have made a commitment.

How does it change?

If you haven't made a commitment, you can blow where the wind blows. You can go wherever your hedonistic, whimsical, opportunistic desires take you. But once you have a path, it's different. For instance, once you have made a commitment with a spouse, you can't enjoy with another person. If you do, you hold your integrity and relationship in jeopardy.

That commitment is a by-product of the experience. Once you have that kind of commitment, whatever you do is an expression of Godliness, and you are not going to quit until it's done.

How is it an expression of Godliness?

In the Hindu story called the *Ramayana*, Hanuman flew to Lanka to find Sita, Rama's wife. In the middle of his jumping to Lanka, Maina Mountain came to Hanuman and said, "Why don't you rest here? The Gods sent me to give you a break." Hanuman said, "Why would I want to rest when I'm working for God? Who wants to rest? It's much more fun and exhilarating to work for God."

What else is it like after the experience of samadhi?

I can only say that I have much more energy, even thirty years later. I have unbounded energy. If I sleep more than three or four hours a night, I feel like I'm wasting time. I get a call in the middle of the night to get to work. I work on a myriad of projects which are all expressions of divinity. I use the talents I have to further the interest of spiritual seekers.

What else would you say the experience is like?

I can't say what is going on with me without having unnecessary diversion in the ego. I'm the same boring, dull guy that makes everybody fall asleep. That's how I'd describe the experience of getting enlightened.

That makes me want to sign up!

There are many teachers who say that we are already enlightened and spiritual practices have the danger of supporting the idea that we need to do something to get there. What do you think of that point of view?

I think that's very true from the standpoint of Vedanta, of unity. If you are in the place of unity, the postulation of requiring a practice to realize the unity is fallacious. However, how many of us stay in this experience? That may be true for Ramakrishna or Ramana Maharshi, but I can't attest to that for myself. All the members of creation that I know are acting and interacting in duality. They need a path and practice to help them experience the unity. I don't think it's fair to say that we are all one, and there's nothing to do, and anything you can do is merely an obstacle. I know intellectually that consciousness is always free, yet my mind has certain attitudes and directions and it doesn't regard all as being in unity all the time. Even the greatest teachers of Vedanta get in an airplane and travel around the world to share their opinions. If there is only unity, who would go where to share what with whom?

The idea that you don't have to do anything to move toward enlightenment may apply to the Satya Yuga, but in this age of activity we have to act. When we act, there are two possibilities: either we act for ourselves or we act for God. So we may as well act in a way that is designed to remind us that we are already enlightened. That's why we suggest there is a need for practices.

10

Becoming Perfect

According to the tradition of sanatana dharma, every atom of existence has come into being to manifest perfection, to manifest the highest ideal of what it can become. The leaf is trying to be the perfect leaf, the sadhu is trying to become the perfect sadhu.

Is that the purpose of life, to become perfect?

Yes. We all have outstanding debts of karma, which is why we took birth. We will continue to take birth until we attain perfection. That means we have no more debts.

What do you mean by perfection? What is perfection for a human being?

The definition of perfection is different for every one of us in every circumstance. We know when we touch perfection.

When people think of perfection, they tend to think of being free of weaknesses, faults and neurotic tendencies. Is that what you mean by perfection?

Absolutely. When you are in that state of union and communion, you are not thinking of the little "I" and its inadequacies and its limitations. You are thinking about the union, about the "we" rather than the "I." Then it becomes an exciting, energizing moment. As we make that moment longer and longer, we begin to live in the state of realization and liberation.

Are you free of faults in that state?

You are free of everything, not just faults. You are free from all attributes. You become nirguna, beyond qualities.

Is it possible for a human being to reach that state?

Absolutely. In the state of samadhi, you reach nirguna bliss. If you can do it in a moment of samadhi, you can do it in a life of samadhi.

You get more and more comfortable and familiar with that state, and it expands into your life more and more?

Yes. You experience being in harmony with everything. When you have a motivation, a particular desire you want fulfilled, then you see everything in terms of your desire. When you have no desire to fulfill, you perceive everyone the same. If you don't need anything, everyone is equal in your eyes. If you have a pressing need, you see some people can fulfill your need and some people can't. Those who can't aren't important to you. So you have an attachment. Do you understand?

Everywhere the pickpocket goes he sees pockets. Your desire creates your universe.

That's right. So if you have no selfish desire, if your desire is only to share love and joy and song, you can share that wherever you go.

Is that the state of a realized being?

Yes. Nothing is pulling you backwards. All your debts are fulfilled.

The rishis were talking about the truth as they saw it thousands of years ago. Were they in touch with an eternal truth that is still applicable today?

Whatever they said is still applicable today if it is eternal. Now they said some things that applied to the mundane world and they said some things that pertained to our relationship with God. They said, "God lives in every atom of existence, and wherever you find energy, you will find consciousness." They said, "God is omnipresent. God is everywhere. So anything you do, at any time, anywhere, you are with God."

Our relationship with God is not going to change. All humankind is comprised of the same elements, and we all inhabit Mother Earth. If we are all children of Mother Earth, then we are all brothers and sisters. That is an eternal truth that is not going to change. If we are all children of God, how can we spend so much time and so many resources

fighting with each other? Because since the dawn of recorded history we have chosen to ignore the truth, we say, "Yes, we are all children of God, but call God by the name that I call God. Live the way I think you should live, and then we will have peace."

Why are humans like that?

That is part of our nature, unfortunately. That is the part of our nature that pushes us into duality. The other part of us strives for unity. That part says, "I am one with God. I am the child of God, and the whole world is my family." The part of us that strives for individuality, the part that wants to be important, that wants to be an authority, is the egotistical force within us that demands that the ego be expressed. He is constantly getting us into trouble.

145

Most people identify with the ego. They think that is who they are.

The egotistical force is the force of attachment, and each one of us is so attached to our desires that we can rationalize any behavior that brings success. Even if our conscience tells us it is wrong, we can rationalize our behavior because it brings us closer to our goals. We see morality and common sense being thrown to the winds in the face of this overpowering desire of our ego for self-aggrandizement. My conscience tells me it's wrong, morality tells me it's wrong, the conventions of society tell me it's wrong. It's against the law, I'm going to do it clandestinely, and still there is something that draws me, almost like a magnetic force, toward the fulfillment of my desires. The irony of it all is that my desires never get fulfilled. Even if I fulfill them for a moment, it is such a transitory elation that I have to do it again.

Why don't we realize this? We strive for a goal, we reach the goal and are happy for a short time, and then it doesn't satisfy us any more. Why don't we realize that this program is not working?

The reason is that we are focusing on the goal, not on the path. When you focus on the goal as the means of fulfillment, then the path is something we have to get out of the way in order to achieve the goal. The path becomes an obstacle. So I can't enjoy the process, because I have to overcome the process to get to my goal. When we find that the process is our sadhana and we enjoy the process, then it doesn't matter if we get to the goal or not. The goal is merely the direction.

I think most people would agree with what you just said. Yes, we should be in the moment. We should enjoy the process. But very few people do that. Why is it so hard?

There are old patterns, old habits of behavior that have become instinctive to us. We were trained from childhood, and that conditioning has created such an intense degree of bondage that it is very, very difficult to escape from it. Our minds slip back, even unconsciously, into old patterns of behavior. But when we love something very much, all the little loves yield to the big love. The thing we love the most we pay the most attention to, and that is the only way to get out of that trap.

How do you learn to love like that?

First you need an inspiration, like a Guru, for instance. Once you find that inspiration, you need to allow yourself the privilege of falling in love. Now, for many years society has been defining what respectable behavior is for us. Suddenly, we find ourselves inspired to follow another course of behavior. We have to forgive ourselves for accepting society's values for so long. Then we have to allow ourselves to cultivate a love affair with our inspiration. We need to have a greater love than all our little, transient desires.

So you have to find something better than what you've got going to want to let go of what you are familiar with?

Absolutely. We are trying to give ourselves the privilege of loving passionately. I don't want to love you intellectually; I want to love you totally, with exuberance, with feeling. The more I get swept up in the feeling of love and joy, the less I think about my "self." This is what we call surrender. I have surrendered my attachments. I have surrendered my egotism. I have surrendered selfishness, because I am in love. Not because someone gave me an ultimatum and put a gun to my head and said, "Surrender or else," but because the joy, the love, the warmth are so overpowering, so desirable that all the little desires pale in comparison. I didn't give up anything. I just pursued what I wanted most!

That sounds like a fun way of doing it.

11

THE SANATANA DHARMA

Previously you mentioned the tradition of sanatana dharma. What is the goal of the sanatana dharma?

The goal is for every atom of existence in its own way to be free from karma and achieve its own state of perfection.

Okay, that's the part I don't understand. Does everything have a different state of perfection?

Yes. The perfection of the atoms of a tree is different from the perfection of the atoms of a human being. If you look at the attitude of a tree, it gives its shade to everyone. It gives its wood for fuel. It gives its flowers for people who like to smell them. It gives its fruit for people to eat. It takes the minimum it needs and grants refuge to everyone.

So the Guru, like the tree, offers to everybody. Come and take what you want. You see a person like Shree Maa, who offers so much to so many.

So back to what the sanatana dharma is, I am trying to put it into a larger context. Does it derive from Ramakrishna's philosophy or from the Vedas or somewhere else?

149

Sanatana dharma is the eternal ideal of perfection. So it was before Ramakrishna. It was before the Vedas. The Vedas are mere expressions of the sanatana dharma. The Vedas are the oldest expressions known to humankind trying to define the sanatana dharma.

How old are the Vedas?

Well, it depends on your perception. There are many people who try to put the Vedas at 3,000 BC. Others would put them at 12,000 or 15,000 BC.

And the sanatana dharma existed even before the Vedas?

The Vedas are the oldest scriptures that talk about sanatana dharma. They are not the sanatana dharma. The sanatana dharma is the eternal ideal of perfection, which predates the Vedas. The Vedas are an attempt to describe these ideals. And it was a very good attempt.

Were the people who wrote the Vedas enlightened beings?

History called them that. I didn't know their physical manifestations personally. They have been a tremendous inspiration to me, and I'm sure they have influenced many thinkers through many millenniums.

The sanatana dharma touches on every aspect of life. It is about how you can manifest perfection in every action you perform. The sanatana dharma is about spiritual life. It's not about practices. Practices are tangential to the main thesis.

They are the tools for reminding ourselves always to be engaged in the spiritual path.

I don't understand the context for this body of teachings.

It's not necessarily a body of teachings, because all the teachings haven't been revealed yet. The difficulty with giving it a historical context is that it limits us to one preconceived idea of spirituality. We are not propagating any religion. It's true that our teachings are Sanskrit-based, and we love the Gods. But we love them all; we pray in many different languages. We have Jesus in our temple and we have Buddha, too.

You're an equal opportunity God lover.

That's right! We love all Gods equally, because they all represent the one God. So I don't want to give a definition that limits the scope of dharma. We are seeking the highest ideal of perfection for every being in every species, and every being will define that ideal for himself or herself.

I am hesitant to talk about dharma in terms of a teaching or a body of knowledge or an "ism" of any kind. The sanatana dharma has nothing to do with religion, even the Hindu religion.

But you use certain spiritual scriptures.

Yes, I do, because I am more familiar and comfortable with Sanskrit than I am with, for instance, Latin.

So the sanatana dharma is too big to limit?

Yes.

As a point of reference for the Western mind, how would you compare the sanatana dharma to Christianity and Buddhism?

Both Jesus and Buddha are examples of the sanatana dharma. They are seers of the eternal ideal of perfection and have translated it into the appropriate terminology for their time, place and circumstance. So I wouldn't make any distinction between the teaching of Buddha and Jesus and the sanatana dharma. However, in Christian-ity or Buddh-ism there are a lot of "thou shalt not's." There are 631 mitzvahs in the book of Leviticus which tell you "thou shalt" do it this way.

The sanatana dharma cannot be limited. We would say that every being will determine and define his or her own ideal of perfection according to their time, place and circumstances. For example, in the books of Genesis and Leviticus you have an allusion to the laws of kosher, which say that you should not mix dairy products with meat products. These rules are very important to the people who live in the desert with no refrigeration. When you go to India, where the Ganges plane is rich and fertile, most people have so many vegetables that they have no need to eat meat. They are practicing ahimsa, which is nonviolence to anyone. They are trying to eat a vegetarian diet. The laws of kosher don't apply to them.

So we can say in each scripture some of the instructions are about our relationship to the world, and some are about our

153

relationship to God. Some of the prescriptions of every scripture are transient, and some of them are eternal. As soon as it becomes an "ism" and an "ity," then it is easy to mix the two and forget our responsibility for discriminating according to our own conscience. That attitude gives birth to religious intolerance.

So that attitude applies to Hinduism, also?

Certainly. There is fundamentalism in every religion. As soon as you have an "ism," you are moving away from the teachings of Jesus or Buddha or Shankaracharya, and you are moving into the codification of laws and prescriptions: "You should do it this way. We will tell you what your ideal of perfection will be." As soon as you say what you should do and what you shouldn't do, you have created a "we — they" situation. Sanatana dharma says, "You will know what your ideal of perfection is."

Relationships With Divinity

12

GODS AND GODDESSES

Could you explain more about the purpose and value of worshiping Gods and Goddesses?

Man went to God and said, "God, we can't remember you all the time. You exist in every aspect of existence, but we don't remember the infinite unmanifest when we are living in the world of manifested reality. Will you please give us a form, so we can have a relationship with you and remember you at least some of the time? Will you give us a time and a place and a special attitude, so that we can cultivate this relationship?" And God said, "I am infinite and beyond conception, symbolized by OM. I exist in every aspect of creation. But because of your devotion, I am going to assume a special form for you. Go down to the river, scoop up some mud, mix it with straw and pray. When your prayer is sufficiently sincere, your attentiveness will bring my form into manifestation. That form, that art, that love, that generosity you exhibit in making my form manifest will bring divinity close to you. It will be a container of your devotion, of all your love, of your longing for a relationship with divinity."

This isn't an idol; this is a symbol. There is a significant difference. A good example of this is the concept of zero. We use it every day. In fact, it is a Hindu concept. It came from India, and none of the functions in life would be efficient without it. The zero doesn't mean anything. It means the absence of everything. Yet because of that symbol, we know what we are talking about. We have agreed to use this symbol to make our communications more efficient.

The image of Kali is the symbol for surrendering darkness. The image isn't the divinity Herself; it is the doorkeeper to the divinity. It opens the door so we can go through this symbol, through this form, into the formless. It is the doorkeeper who opens the door.

Can you have a relationship with that formlessness?

You cannot have a relationship with the unmanifest. You can have a relationship with the doorkeeper and you can intuitively experience, in meditation, the state of nonduality. Relationship implies two. Nonduality means one.

So we have all these doorkeepers that symbolize different paths and relationships. One says surrender your darkness; the other says illuminate your light. Another says fill yourself with joy and wisdom and creativity. Each attitude is another means of relating to the doorkeeper who will take us beyond duality into the state of unity.

How do these dualistic relationships lead to the experience of nonduality?

There is a point in every love affair when we look into the eyes of our beloved and thought ceases. We "grok" each other. There is a knowing, an intuitive understanding that goes beyond the intellect. As Thoreau said, "Sometimes I sit at Walden Pond and cease to be." It is just that simple. We look into the eyes of our beloved with so much intensity that we cease to be two. We exist as one. That is how the gate keeper opens the door. When we love God so much in the form, we merge into the form and become One. Duality ceases to exist.

Once we have an understanding of what we are looking for, it's a lot easier to look for it. Once you have had an experience of samadhi, it is so much easier to put yourself back there. All you do is recount what you were doing when you went there. What did it feel like as you were going? What were you looking to become? How can you let go and just be what you want to become?

There seems to be a Ben and Jerry's variety of Gods in the Eastern tradition. I understand the value of having a symbol of God to relate to, but why not just one symbol? Why thousands?

There is only one God, and everything in existence is a reflection of the image of God; it is part of that God. Any symbol that represents perfection to someone is that person's deity, what we call their ishta deva, their chosen form of worship. Every individual can choose what form they wish to worship. Why is anyone's choice better than anyone else's choice? Therefore, we get a plethora of deities to worship. Why not? It's an individual's relationship with the divine. Why not let every individual choose what kind of relationship he or she wants?

That relationship may evolve in the course of an individual's life. For instance, sometimes we may call the Divine Mother Kali, or She who takes away the darkness of our ignorance. Sometimes we may worship Her as Saraswati, the Goddess who gives knowledge. She is only one Goddess, but according to our different needs as our situation and circumstance in life change, our perception of that deity will change. The monotheistic religions also call God by different names. For instance, in Judaism, God is sometimes called Jehovah, the Lord of Hosts, sometimes Eloheim, the compassionate, merciful God. The Hebrew people are not polytheists, yet they call him by different names according to their different desires.

That sounds similar to the Indian teaching story about the blind men who meet an elephant.

Yes. A number of blind men came upon an elephant, and one man touched the leg and said, "This is like a big pillar," and someone touched his side and said, "This is like a big wall," and someone touched his tail and said, "This is like a slithering snake." Someone touched his trunk and said,

"This is like a creeping vine," and no one really described the elephant.

So if the elephant was God, each could worship the different parts of the elephant and say, "This is my ishta deva. This is what the chosen symbol of God is for me."

Yes. Everyone could try to define the infinite in his or her own way, but who could define the infinite? There is a song Ramakrishna used to sing, "Who can know you unless you allow yourself to be known?" How can we describe the infinite? Can we really say that we have described infinity and know that our form is superior to your form of infinity? Infinity means without limit. How can I define the limitless and say my definition is clearer than yours is? What arrogance. It's a logical fallacy. So Hinduism says, "Yes, every object of manifested existence is divine. It can reflect divinity to anyone who wishes to perceive it. So worship God in any form you choose to see as divine." The point is to worship, practice, meditate, contemplate and remember that there is a divine power which is superior to us.

In addition to being reflections and symbols of divinity, have these Gods and Goddesses walked the earth? Are they personalities, and can we relate to them like we can relate to a Guru? Are they historical characters?

Yes, they are historical characters who did walk on this planet. They are personalities which have manifested in creation. If we were to withdraw our perception from the earth and look at earth from a greater distance with an expanded awareness, we would see the Goddess Saraswati as a separate entity, a being in this universe.

So they are all here, but we just can't see them?

They are too big to see. We can only feel them from this limited perception. If we were to see earth from outer space, we would see one earth and imagine it as a paradise of union. We would see one human race. We wouldn't perceive that humans drew lines across the face of the earth, saying this is China and this is Japan and these are Muslims and these are Hindus, and they are all fighting with each other. We could never perceive that until we landed on earth.

In the same way, when we look for God from this limited perception, we are trying to see God from within our paradigm of reality. Of course, we are going to put God in anthropomorphic terms we can relate to: God is just like me. Whereas if we look at Godliness from the outer reaches of space, we will perceive Godliness in a totally different form.

Can you say more about how you can see it?

No. How can I describe it? But I can tell you it does exist. I have verified that.

So there is a being to have a relationship with. We can't see it, because it's so big...

We can see it if we strive to see it. The way to see it is by looking for God in little things first. Then making God bigger and bigger until we have practiced seeing beyond the limitations of our finite mind. We start to look with our inner eyes. Then we have knowledge to a certainty that this divinity exists as a conscious being and we become conscious of the consciousness.

If we want to have a relationship with divinity in the form of Lakshmi, for instance, can we appeal to and have a relationship with that Goddess? Can we actually see Her?

Yes, we can. We can see Her, we can feel Her, we can touch Her, we can taste Her. She is empirically verifiable. Just as intimately as we are speaking to one another, we can have conversations with God.

Are the pujas part of the technology that allows us to do that?

Yes. The pujas allow us to expand our consciousness to that awareness and cultivate that relationship. We begin by seeing God in little things. We practice seeing God in a flower, in a candle, in an altar of worship, in a form of deity that we put our love and devotion into. Then the relationship increases exponentially.

Why do the Gods and Goddesses look the way they do? Why that form instead of another form? Is there a reason for their appearance?

Yes. Each one of the deities is an embodiment of a whole set of spiritual and philosophical aspirations. They are the embodiment of an entire school of philosophy and a whole set of spiritual practices which is designed to bring us to the realization of that philosophy. So the various arms, weapons and mudras (gestures) are all indicative of aspects of spiritual disciplines.

Is the form symbolic?

Definitely.

Is there also something intrinsic in their appearance? Would different people see the same form independently?

Originally there were many visionaries, rishis, who had the vision of this form of divinity.

Different people had the same vision?

Different people had a perception of the same form. We have said there is one God and that divinity resides in every atom of existence. Just as one woman is a mother to a child and a child to her mother, she is also a friend to her friend. She has many roles. When she goes swimming she wears a swimming suit, and when she goes to work she wears a business suit. That one woman has many different forms, according to her relationships and functions. She has different names, according to the different relationships she has. In the same way, the one God has many names and forms.

162

There seems to be an agreed upon form or appearance for Lakshmi, for instance. Most artists depict her in a similar way. Beyond her symbolism, is the way she looks related to her intrinsic appearance?

The way she looks was originally perceived in the vision of a rishi and it was written down in Sanskrit verse. Later her form was created in accordance with this description of her subtle form.

Was this rishi seeing only his vision of Lakshmi or was he seeing something that other rishis could also see because that is the way that Goddess appears to humankind?

Every form of every divinity intrinsically looks the same to everyone who perceives it, but the way you paint the picture is according to the individual tastes of the artist.

So there is something intrinsic. Is it more of a feeling than the way the Goddess looks?

To the rishis, feelings were objects of perception, just like sounds and smells and colors and tastes. So their perceptions of color and form cannot be separated from their perceptions of feeling. They perceived the feeling and the intrinsic nature of any other being just as you or I would see the extrinsic nature of a being. We look at the external form and say, "I have seen so-and-so." They looked at the external form and internal form. They perceived the essence. So you can't separate the essence from its manifested existence.

If I had a vision of Lakshmi, would I perceive some intrinsic quality that the rishi would also perceive, but because of my background and culture, I would see something different?

Yes. It would be like describing the color of the red on the bottoms of her feet. Some would say it's a deep red, some magenta, some would say it's a light red. Or a better example is to describe how sweet is sweet. When you try to describe it, of course, words are going to fail you, because my understanding may be different from yours.

Many people pray to the Goddess for a better job or for children or more money. What is the value of this kind of prayer? If it is your karma not to have children, how does prayer affect your karma?

There are four types of devotion. Tamasic devotion seeks to injure someone else by one's prayer to God: "Please, God, destroy my enemies." Rajasic devotion seeks to attain something for oneself: "Give me wealth, give me children." Now these two forms of devotion are selfish and may or may not lead to sattvic devotion, which says, "Lord, make me an instrument of your peace." The fourth type of devotion is called parabhakti, the supreme devotion, which says, "God, I love you! I am so pleased to be able to sit here and tell you how much I love you." In the first two forms of devotion, God is forgotten when the objective is attained. In the last two forms of devotion, God is being remembered daily.

Lakshmi

As I understand karma, your actions create certain results. So let's say there are certain results that are coming to you from your previous actions. Does praying change those results?

Yes. In many ways it assists the individual to feel that God is on their side. The power that comes from feeling that we are being blessed allows us to move forward with renewed vigor. We have more strength and courage. We have a different energy and a different attitude that makes things work better. Every time we take the name of God, we get a blessing.

And that blessing would change our karma?

Certainly it does.

13
WHAT IS A GURU?

Who or what is the Guru?

"Gu" means darkness, and "ru" means the illuminator of light. "Guru" means someone who will illuminate my darkness. It may be an individual or several individuals. Gurus are the teachers who inspire us and exemplify the most wonderful conduct we can perform while in a human body. They motivate and show us how to come closer to our ideals of perfection.

If a Guru exemplifies absolute truth...

Or even a relative truth. We don't have to look for total perfection in an individual. It would be enough to see someone who knows how to worship purely. Why do we need the perfect Guru? We all have so many Gurus. I had one person teach me how to read and another how to solve math problems. I have had many teachers. Some are perfect in one subject. I don't know anyone who is perfect in all subjects.

Aren't there some beings who are perfect in the sense that they are fully realized?

Even if they are perfectly realized, they are perfect in some ways and imperfect in other ways.

But if they have reached the goal of perfection, aren't they perfect?

In some ways. In the way that they have produced effort to manifest Godliness. I will give you a very close example. Shree Maa radiates a tremendous amount of perfection. She radiates love and service through her every action. She is constantly thinking of other people. However, she is not perfect in maintaining her body.

Is this kind of imperfection a consequence of being born into a body?

Of course. If you have a body, you have some limitations. You may have reached perfection in consciousness, you may have reached perfection in worship, you may have reached perfection in many fields you are interested in, but that doesn't mean you are perfect in everything.

When a divine being manifests in a body, what are the conditions he or she must deal with? What comes with the package?

Everybody has an obligation to maintain his or her body. They have a natural tendency to preserve that body. They have to clothe the body, feed the body and house the body. They have relationships because of the body. They are born into certain families that are most conducive for them to achieve their goals. They have siblings and relations that create the environment that is needed for them to pursue their ideals of perfection. Someone who has a degree of realization still has the constraints of the body.

What about a personality? Is that part of being born on earth?

Absolutely. Everybody has a personality. Most of the personality traits are conditioned. You are born in a certain ethnic stock that has a certain language and mode of expression, and that shapes the personality.

You are saying that a divine being would have preferences, even though the divine state is beyond preferences. That seems like a paradox.

Shree Maa, in her childhood, ate boiled rice with a little mashed potato and a spoonful of ghee and some salt. That was her breakfast for all the years of her childhood. Now that she is advanced in years, her natural tendency is to have boiled rice for breakfast. I tried many times to give her toast for breakfast, and she would take one bite and get up and make her boiled rice. She prefers to have the food to which she has become accustomed. That is an attitude of the body which was conditioned. It has nothing to do with enlightenment or liberation. But it came from her environment, and she maintains that tradition.

Is that why it can become confusing when you see a Guru demonstrating a preference? They say, "I don't like artichokes," and you think, "How could they not like artichokes? They are supposed to love everything." Are you saying that independent of their divinity there is a personality that has nothing to do with who they really are?

That is correct. It has nothing to do with their degree of enlightenment either. The fact that they don't like artichokes has nothing to do with the wisdom they have attained.

Would you say that the difference between an average person and an enlightened person is that the enlightened person doesn't identify with their preferences? They don't think they are their likes and dislikes.

That's true, but there's more. A realized being sees that the God within you is the God within me. If I lift you up in any way, I am doing good to myself and I am doing good to my world. It benefits me to do good to others. It is all me.

That is another statement that you hear a lot: "We are all One. The God in you is the God in me." To most people that just sounds like a lot of words.

It sounds like platitudes until you come to really feel it. The more you cultivate the love affair with people who have the

feeling, the closer you come to the feeling. So in the Devi Mandir (Shree Maa and Swami's ashram), we put in eighteen- to twenty-hour days. And people say, "What do you do to have fun?" and I say, "This is fun! This is the life I chose. I am not doing this because I have to."

If the Guru is enlightened, would they have thoughts?

Well, the Guru moves in and out of enlightenment, just like a sadhu moves in and out of samadhi. You can't stay there all the time. There are two parts to the equation. One is to realize the highest divinity, and the other is to share it with whomever we can.

Do you have to have thoughts to share it?

Certainly. How can you move somewhere to share wisdom without duality? Who will share what with whom?

Isn't there a samadhi where you are moving around?

I think you're referring to sahaja samadhi. It doesn't mean samadhi in terms of full absorption. It means behind the facade of the physical manipulations in this world, we simultaneously see the stage of consciousness upon which all this drama is being manifest. You see the backdrop of divinity. But that's not the same as samadhi where you don't see any distinctions.

What is the difference between an Upa Guru and a Sat Guru?

Any teacher is an Upa Guru. They show us the stepping stones along the way. Sat Gurus demonstrate and embody the highest fulfillment for us. They coordinate the teachings we get from all of our Upa Gurus. They are our root Guru.

Is there only one Sat Guru for each person?

There is one highest ideal of perfection. We would suggest that the Sat Guru of all Sat Gurus is Lord Shiva. He is the Guru of all Gurus.

Ramana Maharshi said, "God, Guru and Self are one." Could you explain what that means?

The Guru is the purest being on earth that I can think of. God is the purest essence of all existence. The Self, which is consciousness, is totally pure once it has divested itself of selfish thoughts. So when we strive to reduce our selfishness, we come closer to the example that the Guru exemplifies and we come closer to God.

You said, "Closer to God," but the saying is God, Guru and Self are the same.

At some point, we will recognize that our Guru is divinity made manifest on earth. We will recognize that our consciousness, when unencumbered, is one with the Guru.

13
HAVING A RELATIONSHIP WITH YOUR GURU

Does loving a Guru make you more like him or her?

Yes. The more I love my Guru, the more I want to know about my Guru. What makes her happy? What does she like to eat? Where does she like to go? What kind of flowers does she like? How can I love her more? Wouldn't I do that for a friend? Wouldn't I do that for a lover? Why won't I do that for God?

How does knowing what the Guru likes lead you anywhere?

It leads me to pleasing my beloved, and the more my beloved is pleased with me the more inspiration I get to love more. I want to love more, because she is so pleased. Then the love grows more and more until we want to jump up and shout!

But that's not all. I don't only want to please the Guru; I want to emulate her. I love the Guru so much that I want to be

like her. I want to learn about what she is doing and why she is doing it so I can do it too.

You do the same thing that the Guru is doing and then you become more and more like the Guru?

That's right. That's the example I want to follow. My love becomes what Aristotle called "entellichi," the inner urge to become something greater. There is this attraction that pulls me magnetically to want to improve. So I have this magnetic attraction to my Guru that says, "I want to be like that. I respect that individual so much that I don't just want to please them, I want to become like them."

175

That is the difference between a devotee and a disciple. The devotee says, "I want to please the Guru." The disciple says, "I want to become the reflection of the Guru." In Sanskrit, the term for disciple is "shishya," which means mirror. You look in the mirror and you can't tell which is the original and which is the reflection. That's the relationship between Guru and disciple. The relationship between Guru and devotee is the devotee comes to please the Guru, but doesn't necessarily make changes in his or her life. They hold on to the same old baggage that they're carrying around, even while they are trying to please the Guru. The disciple automatically polishes their image so that it reflects in the same way the Guru's image reflects.

Why do Indians bow down to their Guru? From a Western point of view, that can seem disempowering.

It isn't. The greatest power comes from knowledge, and true knowledge bestows humility. Every time we humble ourselves we are empowering ourselves, because we put ourselves in an attitude conducive to receiving blessings.

King Dasharatha went to see a rishi to get a blessing in order to have children. So the Queen said, "Prepare the procession so we can travel to see the rishi." Dasharatha said, "No, no, my Queen. When someone goes to receive a blessing, they don't go with a full vessel to demonstrate their wealth. They go with an empty vessel to hold the blessing." So he went alone and barefoot, without a crown on his head, to ask for a blessing.

Every time we bow down, we humble ourselves. Jesus said, "Let the greatest amongst you be a servant." He also said, "When you go to a host, always take a lower seat and allow the host to move you to a higher seat of honor."

In this way, if we make ourselves humble, we empower ourselves to receive knowledge. If you go to a Guru, go to learn, not to teach. If the cup is full, then no more can go in. There are many people who want to tell a Guru everything they know so the Guru can understand what to teach. A Guru will never teach such a person. One must go with a question.

The problem I think many people may have when they hear this is that they have experienced surrendering to another person and they've been hurt, manipulated and taken advantage of.

This is something different. We are talking about surrendering to God and using that other person as a vehicle to get to God.

What about Gurus who have been inappropriate and have abused people in various ways in this country? Some of us may be afraid to love an enlightened being because that person may be a phony and take advantage of us.

Many of the people who found themselves abused relinquished their discrimination. Gurus are humans, too.

But that's a tough call, isn't it? My guess is that most people don't think they would know an enlightened being from their

Uncle Bernie. So they think, "I don't know, and this wise being seems to know, so I'll follow his truth."

I doubt that. I believe the people who think they don't know say, "I'm going to watch." That's discrimination. If a person said to a Guru, "I want to love you because you exemplify Godliness," then they would keep it all on a divine level. But many people said, "I want to possess this Godliness and attach myself to it as I would to any other worldly love." When they said that, they failed to discriminate between what is going to take them closer to God and what is just a transient enjoyment. They were not surrendering themselves selflessly, or they wouldn't have felt taken advantage of.

Let's say someone fell in love with a Guru and they wanted to be unselfish and they said to the Guru, "I will give you all of my money." Then they found out that the Guru used the money to buy a Rolls Royce. Wouldn't that be an example of someone who was approaching the relationship unselfishly but still got taken advantage of?

As W.C. Fields said, "There's a sucker born every minute." The fact that we are longing to be spiritual doesn't absolve us from the responsibility to watch and discriminate. We are not absolved from responsibility because we hope that this person is going to be the messiah.

So this surrender and passionate love you are talking about comes after you have really checked the Guru out?

No, it comes even in the process of checking the Guru out. But even if I surrender to you totally, that doesn't mean you get to take everything and I don't get anything. That's not surrender. In Sanskrit the term is "samarpana." "Sama" means equilibrium, and "arpana" means to offer: I offer myself with total equilibrium. So we must look to see that it is a reciprocal relationship. In fact, spirituality means giving more than we take. A real Guru always gives more than they take. Shree Maa, for instance, is always giving to everyone, and she never asks for anything in return.

What other qualities should we look for when observing a Guru?

If one teaching is taught in public and another in private, I would be suspect. Secondly, if a Guru is married and wants to give tantric initiation to single women, I would be concerned about sexual abuse.

A true Guru is a giver. The preponderance of his talks are inspiring, knowledgeable and uplifting. The attitude of his life conveys respect. He speaks with authority and without manipulation. A true Guru will pay respect to ancient wisdom. He will use the scriptures and the lives of other rishis and saints as examples of behavior to emulate.

Their teachings wouldn't be focused exclusively on themselves, like they have the only way.

Right. True Gurus won't call attention to themselves. They'll call attention to the masters that preceded them. True

Gurus have a lineage and a heritage. They'll talk about art, culture, history, psychology, and yet they will direct discussions away from day-to-day concerns. Their home is not of this world. They carry themselves as renunciates. They demonstrate faith in the practice of sadhana.

Do they still practice?

They do. They practice to demonstrate to others how to maintain their shine.

When we are in a romantic love affair, there are different stages. After the honeymoon stage, our feelings usually diminish, and we go back to our normal reality. Are there also rhythms in our love affairs with God or Guru?

There don't have to be. However, there can be stages for those of us who have fickle minds and are waiting to be entertained by our lovers. Those who have selfish attachment have selfish love affairs. For those who are unselfish, there isn't a honeymoon period. It's all just bliss. To be in the presence of our Guru, to be in the presence of God, is just as rewarding after many years as it was on the first day.

Now it's true that there are three gunas in nature: sattva, rajas and tamas. These three gunas are attributes and qualities of nature. The three gunas are in constant transformation. Even though they all exist at the same time, at any point one is predominant over the others. There is a cyclical transformation between the gunas. For instance, when new knowledge arises in the sattva state, we want to manifest that knowledge, and that urges us to rajas. After a period of activity, it's time to take rest, and that's tamas. After we have rested, we want to start learning again, and that's sattva.

How does that process manifest itself while falling in love with the Guru?

When falling in love with our beloved, we want to learn all about her. In the sattvic stage, we are learning all about our beloved. When we find out what kind of behavior is appreciated by our beloved, then we move into a rajasic period when we start manifesting the activity we think will be pleasing to our beloved. Then we take rest. All three are necessary.

Isn't sattva preferable to tamas?

No. Tamas is rest, and rest allows rejuvenation. So it's all part of nature. Everything in existence is subject to the three gunas.

What do you do when you are feeling tamasic and you don't have the energy to pursue wisdom?

Give yourself the space to rejuvenate. Look at yourself and see if this lack of energy is part of your natural rhythm or if you're just being lazy. If you're just being lazy, then you want to manage your tamas so you don't create greater problems for anybody, including yourself. If you are angry or negative, then it might be prudent to find someone to share it with in a positive way, or to get good feedback, or to just take some rest or nourishment. Change your scene so you don't explode and pollute your environment with negativity. That will make a bigger problem for you.

Now when we have rejuvenated ourselves, let's find something that is worthy of devoting our energy to. That's what the Guru will help us to do. The Guru will give us an example of how to channel our energy effectively. The Guru will give us wise counsel and advice, so when we are confronted with the feelings of tamas we won't express them in damaging ways and make a bigger mess for ourselves. The Guru will show us how to harmonize our rhythms so we can move with the forces of tamas, rajas and sattva and not fight against them.

How do you find a Guru?

First we have to prepare ourselves to be a disciple. We have to create within ourselves a sincere longing to learn and to accept the example presented to us. Dattatreya was so attuned to life and wanted the Guru so badly that he saw the Guru in the form of animals and plants and birds and fish. Many of us are looking for one individual who walks on water. That's not really the Guru.

The principle of Guru is the universal consciousness that resides in every atom of existence. There are certain individuals who have taken birth who manifest that characteristic more than others. Some people are extremely devoid of selfishness and they manifest the ideals of perfection that we could strive to attain.

For every desire there is a Guru to show the means to its attainment. If we desire to be a successful entrepreneur, we can find a Wall Street Guru, and if we desire to experience the highest ideals of perfection, we can find that kind of Guru as well.

What we call enlightened beings, history called rishis or prophets. Their words were written down with great reverence and were called scriptures. So if we are interested in what other enlightened beings did in the past, we could study scriptures, and that would immediately bring us into contact with other people who study scripture. As we meet these students of scripture, automatically we will gravitate towards the influences we need for our most positive development.

So you will find some form of teacher?

Yes. Our network will grow until we find the being who demonstrates the fulfillment of our aspiration, and that will be our Guru.

How do you know if someone is your Guru?

How do you know when you fall in love? You have to have a relationship with your Guru. A relationship with a Guru is not an intellectual relationship. It is a love affair. When you feel in love, you know that is your Guru. When her words and her behavior are in harmony, when you find that her attitudes are ones that you respect and wish to emulate, then you have found your Guru.

15
MOM

Why do you call Shree Maa "Mom"?

Because she's the Mother of the Universe. At least, she is to me. She's my mother. She's my mom.

Can you explain what that means?

I can explain what it means to me, but understand I am talking from my perspective and experience only. Shree Maa does not have a selfish bone in her body. She walks on the grass in such a way it seems the grass bows when it's stepped on. She has so much humility that you might not even notice her if she were sitting in a crowd. She carries herself with such poise and such grace that she makes herself diminutive. I think her attitudes, her service, her love, her guidance, her wisdom, her joy, her light, her music, her cooking are all directed towards making this universe a better place. Every activity she performs on earth is directed towards lifting someone else up. She is constantly thinking of others and never thinking of herself. In this sense, having no selfishness, she has merged with

Godliness. She is an emblem of Godliness. She is the manifestation of Godliness as it would come into the human body. This is the attitude from which she performs every function on earth.

She is one with divinity.

And that's what motivates her and inspires her to behave in this way.

She has no ego or sense of separateness.

She feels herself to be the Mother of the Universe and acts like it. I watch her actions on this earth and I know she's the Mother of the Universe. She acts like it, all the time.

When she says that she is the Mother of the Universe, does she mean that there aren't other Mothers of the Universe?

Of course not. She is not saying, "I am the only Mother of the Universe." She is showing us what we can all become.

Planet Earth

16

HUMAN BIRTH

Why do you consider human birth the highest birth?

Humanity has a capacity to reason. Humans have the capacity to dedicate their minds to the contemplation of whatever their desired objective is. In so doing, they can perform sadhana and realize their total potential.

When you are talking about human beings, are you just talking about beings on this planet?

No.

When you say enlightenment, do you mean just one level of enlightenment?

No.

So what's so great about the body?

You need a body to perform action. This body gives us a vehicle through which we can perform sadhana.

But since meditation is in the mind, why do you need a body?

To carry your mind around. It would be difficult to perform sadhana if you couldn't take your mind from place to place.

Why do you need a body to carry around the mind? What's the body? It's just a lump of clay, right?

No, it's the residence of the soul. We have three levels of consciousness: the gross body, the subtle body and the causal body. The subtle body is called the mind, the world of thoughts, ideas and dreams. The causal body knows the totality, and that allows enlightenment. When the causal body merges into the universal, you become one with God. You become a jivanmukta, liberated while in the body. If you have no body, how can you become liberated?

What happens to the subtle body and causal body when you leave your physical body?

The subtle body contains the samskaras, the tendencies that formulate your next birth. It attaches itself to the causal body.

Isn't there an astral body?

That's the subtle body.

So there is something that happens between births.

190

Yes. There is something that transmigrates between death and rebirth.

Why can't you perform sadhana between births, then?

There is no sadhana to do then, because you have no tools to do it with. The state of mind you had when you left is the state of mind you will have when you reenter.

Everything stops?

Yes. You stop evolving. There is no karma. What will you perform karma with?

You have to have a body to do that?

How can you perform any action without a body?

How about mental action?

Does mental action affect anything?

Yes, thoughts affect things.

They only have an effect to the degree that they are communicated, expressed or manifested in some way.

If I am thinking something about you, doesn't that affect you?

I'd have to have a body to know it.

Okay, back to human birth. Is human birth the right term for anyone in a body?

No. I would use the term manifested existence.

Is the term "human" used solely for people on this planet?

Yes. It's a certain species.

So there are other forms of manifested existence on other planets, and you wouldn't call them human?

No. We might call them aliens.

When you say human birth is the best place for enlightenment, you aren't making a comparison with birth on other planets. You just mean it's the best place compared with animal birth or not having a body at all.

Right. There may be more conducive planets for enlightenment.

Okay, on to another important topic. What is the purpose of suffering?

The purpose of suffering is to teach us how to remember God. When we feel pain, most people will say, "Oh, God, save me from pain. I don't want this." So we immediately increase our relationship with God. If we can experience pain as a tool to stop thinking about our little, personal afflictions and focus instead on God, we can transcend the pain and see it as another thought of the mind. If we can absorb our mind in God, we can train ourselves to be ready for God at the time of going.

If you remember God all the time, would you feel less suffering because there would be no purpose for having pain?

Yes. You might have the same sensations, but the experience will be, "I'm not suffering. I am experiencing the fact that the body feels pain, but I don't suffer because I am experiencing the love of God. The body has pain, but I'm not the body. I am the instrument of God."

There is a famous proverb in Sanskrit that says, "Pain is our teaching, and pleasure is our examination." If we can remember God when we're feeling pleasure, we have really conquered our attachments to this material world.

Why is there so much suffering on this planet?

A long time ago, all the pure souls went to the mountain top to contemplate God and they didn't propagate the species. Who made children? The people who had worldly desires. Those people got caught up in the treadmill of having to provide for and protect their families. So each succeeding generation was created more by the souls who were more attached to the world. Those samskaras went from generation to generation, and by default the purer samskaras were excluded from the new generations.

So there was a greater density of sadhus at one point?

Yes. But the violent souls would fight, and the sadhus wouldn't. So the violent souls killed, and the sadhus said, "The self cannot be killed nor can it kill. The way of truth is one universal spirit."

But on the physical plane...

On the physical plane, most of them were killed.

That implies that the dark forces overcame the light.

That's right. The dark force won.

Isn't the force of light supposed to win?

(Laughing) May the force be with you. The force of light said, "We see only God." Remember the story of Rama and Lakshman? They went to the shore of the lake to bathe, and Rama stuck his arrow into the sand. When they came back, they pulled out the arrow and saw there was blood on the tip of it. When they uncovered the area, they saw that the arrow had pierced the heart of a frog. Rama said, "Frog, why didn't you cry out to me? We could have tried to save you." The frog said, "If a snake were to grab me, I would call, 'Rama, please save me.' But here Rama is killing me himself, so whom should I call? I surrender."

These sadhus were like the frog. They said, "Why should I fight? It's not wrong to be taken advantage of, but it's wrong to take advantage of others."

So that's why we're in the mess we are today.

That's right. That's why there is increasingly greater violence within humanity.

Is this the lila?

This is the lila, the divine drama.

Western psychology doesn't acknowledge those aspects of us that we bring into this birth from previous lifetimes. They assume that all of the person is shaped by its environment and genetic makeup. Would the sanatana dharma say that you come in with more than that?

Certainly. We come in with our samskaras, our tendencies. We also come in with three debts of karma: to the Gods, to the ancestors and to the Gurus. We discharge our debt to the Gods by making this world a better place for our having been here. We discharge our debts to the ancestors by respecting the elders the way we would like to be respected when we are old and by nurturing the young people, teaching them the way we would like the world to become. We discharge our debt to the Gurus, all the teachers who gave us a piece of the puzzle from life to life, from birth to birth, by living in accordance with their wisdom.

Who are the ancestors?

The lineage of the family in which you are born.

Spiritual lineage?

Our material lineage: your parents, grandparents, their grandparents.

Are the spiritual lineage and material lineage connected?

Absolutely. You as an individual have a certain spiritual orientation that you are required to manifest. You come into birth in a family that provides an environment that is most conducive to you expressing that orientation.

If I am from Ramakrishna's lineage, does that mean that my parents are connected to that lineage?

No, that means that your parents are capable of providing you with a launching pad for you to explore that lineage. When we talk about lineage, we mean the environment that allows you to move into your dharma.

I could look into my childhood and see lots of things that did not seem conducive to my spiritual growth. How could that be a launching pad for moving into my dharma?

Those experiences that were not conducive made you flee material life and go out and search for more spiritual fulfillment.

Would you say on some level I chose those parents?

Yes, you chose them because in some way they were conducive to your spiritual growth.

If we are close to people in this lifetime, does that mean that we have known them in another lifetime?

Very possibly, and that is what drew us to that relationship.

17
LEAVING THE BODY

We all come back each lifetime. In fact, we don't even go away.

What do you mean by that?

Energy never dies; it only changes form. Kinetic energy becomes potential energy, and potential energy becomes kinetic. Consciousness never dies. Consciousness is eternal. Each individual is made of consciousness and energy. If the consciousness doesn't die and the energy doesn't die, what dies? If there is not a death, there can't be a rebirth. There is one, continuous transformation. Consciousness and energy are constantly changing forms. You were small when you were a young child, now you are older, someday you will leave this form, and the energy and consciousness will leave this form. What died? What was born?

What about a soul?

The Atma (individual soul) is one with the Paramatma (universal soul). The space inside the container is exactly the same as the space outside the container. The only difference between the two is the definition that is created by the container.

Does that container maintain itself from lifetime to lifetime?

The energy of that container will move into a new container. And the space within the container will move into a new container.

After you let go of this body, is the soul no longer in existence in the same form?

The soul never had a form. The soul is the same as the space. The space is the same inside and outside. When the body dissolves, the container dissolves. The awareness is one with the universal awareness, the world soul, the Paramatma, the Supreme soul. Now here comes a new container that encompasses another piece of that soul. Certainly, all the samskaras, all of the tendencies laden with that soul and that container, are coming into manifestation as a new container of that same consciousness.

What are samskaras?

Samskaras are tendencies, attitudes, a propensity to manifest in a certain way.

Is that what we call ourselves?

Yes.

Do those tendencies maintain some continuity from lifetime to lifetime?

They do.

You used the word "soul" before. The Buddhists don't refer to a soul. Is this a fundamental difference or just semantics?

It is semantics. There is Hinayana and Mahayana Buddhism. I am not a Buddhist scholar, so I am not qualified to speak from a Buddhist point of view. However, in the *Tibetan Book of the Dead*, for example, you have references to the transmigration of the soul.

Is there awareness when you leave the body?

Yes. Awareness doesn't cease to exist.

What do you mean by awareness?

We are calling consciousness the capacity for recognition. The greatest analogy we can use is a mirror. No matter where I hold a mirror, it reflects a reflection. In fact, when most people look in a mirror, they see the reflection. Very few look in the mirror and see the mirror. The mirror is consciousness; the reflection is the nature or the attitude of consciousness which is being reflected. In the same way, awareness is this capacity to reflect and recognize. For example, if you put elements into a test tube, you will find that two atoms of hydrogen will always seek out one atom of oxygen and they make H_2O, water. There is consciousness in the atoms.

I'm completely lost.

Consciousness is the capacity of recognition.

Recognizing what?

Anything. Either similarities or disparities.

When you have consciousness, you are aware. Is that the same as the witness?

It's like the witness. However, a witness doesn't act. When you have two atoms of hydrogen and one of oxygen, you have awareness that is followed by activity. As soon as they recognize each other, they are drawn to each other. In fact, that is pure, unselfish love. There is no other motivation than to unite. In the same way, this consciousness, this capacity to recognize who is suitable to unite with, is in our genes. Every atom in our physical body recognizes every other atom it unites with, and they unite and form a molecule. Then all the molecules recognize the other molecules, and they form a substance. The substance forms organs and the various systems, like the circulatory system. When a foreign atom enters into the system, the system says, "You don't belong here. You're a germ. Call out the white lymphocytes and escort him out of here." These are tendencies of the body to act in a certain way. In the same way, we have developed tendencies in this lifetime to make our contribution to society in a certain way.

Are you talking about personality?

Yes. Personality, talent, skills.

Is consciousness connected to what we call divinity?

202

It is. Consciousness, a pure mirror that is unencumbered by thoughts, is the closest thing to the divine mirror, divine consciousness. So if we can erase all the selfishness from our thoughts, then our consciousness individually will reflect the universality just as the supreme consciousness does. Then our thoughts won't bind us to ego.

So thoughts can either take us toward ego or take us toward consciousness?

Yes. If the thoughts identify with the world, they enhance ego. If they take us toward God, they diminish the ego. So the objective of all our sadhana and all our practices is to cultivate the tendency to think without selfishness, to think about God.

Thoughts are like a cloud that hides consciousness. When they are devoid of selfishness, they are more transparent. Consciousness cannot be seen until the thoughts contain only Godliness, whereupon they become totally transparent and allow us to perceive the one, pure consciousness.

How do we make our thoughts more selfless?

The first thing we can do is our spiritual practices: yoga, pranayama, puja, singing about God. All the practices we do are designed to make us think more about God and less about the world. We just think about loving God, not about all the rewards we'll get when we have attained the goal.

You make a distinction between the world and God, one being more selfish and one without selfishness. But can't you think about the world in an unselfish way?

Certainly. What we are distinguishing is between selfish, worldly thoughts, like "What's in it for me?", and acting in the world without selfishness.

I'm still not clear how consciousness relates to the ego.

When we have a recognition, the ego says, "I am aware." The union between consciousness and its object of perception creates ego, the concept of "I": "I think, therefore I am." Whenever we have this "I," we have separation. We think we are different from others.

If you don't have ego and are pure awareness, are you just noticing whatever is happening?

Yes.

When we leave our body, do we no longer have an ego?

We have a very subtle form of ego, because we have samskaras.

Is the ego commenting on awareness?

No, the ego does not comment. According to our tradition, Purusha and Prakriti reside above the antah-karana, the inner cause. The antah-karana is comprised of four things: ego, manah (subjective thought), buddhi (objective thought) and chitta (all thought, subjective and objective). Objective thoughts are the nouns and verbs of experience: "This is a tree." Subjective thoughts are the adjectives and adverbs of experience: "This is a pretty tree." Chitta is all the stored memories of all subjective and objective thought.

What is ego?

Ego is the sense of "I": "I am separate and different from something else."

Is enlightenment not having that sense of "I"?

Yes.

But you still have thoughts?

In the state of enlightenment, you don't have thoughts. You have thoughts after the state of enlightenment has passed.

Are there thoughts when you leave your body?

No. Just consciousness, a subtle form of ego and samskaras.

Then what happens?

Consciousness will seek the appropriate means of manifesting those tendencies.

18

BETWEEN BIRTHS

What happens in our astral or subtle body between births?

It waits for the appropriate time and then it moves back into a physical body.

There is no learning at all?

What would you learn?

I understood there was learning between bodies.

There is learning, but the only learning is of the universal, not the learning of the individual, because there are no individuals.

You don't have an experience of individuality at all?

No.

So you leave your body and you merge with the universal soul?

Yes, to the extent to which you are capable, and then you manifest again.

Why do you manifest again?

Because you have outstanding karmas, samskaras, tendencies which will cause you to find another conducive environment so that you can act out those desires and tendencies.

When you talk about finding another conducive environment, you're not just talking about a body on earth, right? There are many choices of bodies.

Absolutely.

Is there an experiencer between lifetimes?

Yes.

And that experiencer is experiencing cosmic consciousness?

Yes.

Which is what you talked about experiencing in samadhi?

Yes. I experienced that there was no limit to me. So if we leave the body with tendencies to unite with God and have no desires left to be fulfilled on earth, then there is a chance that we won't come back. Then we can remain in cosmic consciousness.

The test of a sadhu is not during her lifetime, but it's at her death. What does she remember?

And her ability to remember is the accumulation of everything she has learned in her life?

And her ability to be free from any encumbrance or any desire.

From my point of view, right now, remaining in cosmic consciousness seems more scary than attractive. So that's why I keep coming back?

That's why you keep circumambulating the wheel of life.

If I experienced samadhi or cosmic consciousness enough while I'm living on this planet, then I would say that it is attractive?

You would.

Then I'd want to hang out in cosmic consciousness?

You might, or you might say, "I want to come back again and again to help all sentient beings achieve it." You could say, "I want to be one with God all the time, or a servant of God all the time and serve Her in any capacity She chooses."

Merging with God from the point of view of the mind doesn't sound so good, because "I" won't be here anymore.

There are many disciplines that seek to have a heaven where you will find all the enjoyments which you denied yourself on earth.

Shree Maa talks about heaven.

Yes, but she's talking about it from a different point of view.

What does she mean?

Heaven is in the here and now.

You didn't answer the question about the "I" not being here anymore. I think most humans would have this thought, "If I merge with God, I'm not going to be here anymore."

When you merge with God, you are here. But you're not here in a limited capacity. You're here as infinity. You don't cease to exist. You don't destroy the ego. You expand the ego until it becomes the embodiment of all existence.

Your experience of that was so wonderful that you want to keep coming back for more.

Yes, or I want to keep serving God so I can be on Her list, so when She passes out those experiences again, I'm in line.

What happens in between lives for people who aren't ready for merging with God?

They develop a samskara, a tendency, that says, "I want greater pleasure in my life. I want a manifestation with greater enjoyment, free from pain." Or they may have inflicted pain on others, and their karma says, "I want pain inflicted on me." They may go to cosmic consciousness and say, "I don't belong here. I don't feel comfortable here. I want to manifest again so I can work out my karma," and they will, right away.

Often they don't even get to cosmic consciousness. They just move to some type of purgatory where they wait for the next environment that is conducive for them. How long they will wait, I can't say.

Their expectations and thoughts create their experience in between lifetimes. If these thoughts are unpleasant, you can create your own hell, or you can experience cosmic consciousness.

Yes. The hell is created because we are going to search for another gross body so we can complete our karma. We are going to search for a body that has the capacity to fulfill our inclinations. When we speak of hell or confusion, it is the stress and strain of searching for an appropriate body to fulfill our desires, not that we go into any kind of purgatory or inferno, as Dante described.

Why is that stressful?

If you're looking for something and not finding it, you feel dissatisfied. Now, it could be hard to find or it could be very easy to find, depending on our karma.

So the better the karma, the easier it is to find the right body.

Yes, because you know what you are looking for.

In the book Autobiography of a Yogi, *Yogananda's Guru, Shri Yukteshwar, appears before him in a Bombay hotel room and tells Yogananda about other realms one can go to when you leave your body. Muktananda talks about the siddha loka, where siddhas go after they leave their body.*

210

These are described as heavenly realms. How does that fit into what you are saying?

The ishta, the chosen beloved one, exists inside the worshiper as well as outside the worshiper. When we talk about the siddha loka, we are talking about something that is inside us as a state of consciousness. It is not an external physical place. It is a paradigm of reality, a way of looking at experience without the imposition of the ego.

What about the popular idea that your loved ones or God in your chosen form will greet you when you leave your body?

That can happen in cosmic consciousness.

So when we leave our body, we can be in cosmic consciousness and we can be with our Guru?

Yes.

Is it all happening at one time?

It doesn't have to be either/or. For example, one can maintain cosmic consciousness and still function in the universe.

And take another body?

Take another body and still be in the heavenly space with their Guru. Shree Maa is such an individual. Her guru is Ramakrishna. She is with him. She resides in cosmic consciousness. Yet she wears a body and acts and interacts in the world. All three are going on simultaneously.

Once I heard you say that Shree Maa is in touch with all seven planes of consciousness at the same time.

Yes. But she can only communicate to others about one plane at a time.

What are the seven planes of consciousness?

The gross body, perceivable through the senses; the subtle body, conceivable in the mind; the causal body, known through intuition or meditation; the great body of all existence, all that is knowable; the body of all knowledge, which we call the logos; the body of all light, which is the source of all knowledge; the body of true existence, consciousness and bliss. Each plane is more subtle than the next. We become more and more subtle, finer, lighter.

Wow. So when Shri Yukteshwar was talking about the gross, astral and causal worlds, there are four more levels beyond that.

Yes. Lighter and lighter realms.

Is it also infinite?

It becomes infinitely finer and finer until you reach the infinite beyond description, which is symbolized by the term OM.

That's cool.

Pretty fine.

Last question. How do you know that reincarnation occurs?

I personally accept five types of verification that are discussed in the Nyaya philosophy: 1) direct perception, 2) deductive reasoning, 3) inductive logic, 4) testimony, 5) intuitive cognition.

In India, I had demonstrative proof that I had been there before. This proof included my affinity towards the Sanskrit literature, my capacity with Indian languages, my comfort with Indian customs, my ability to absorb Indian scriptures and a lot more. So all five types of verification occurred. That means I must have been reborn.

19

Money And Debt

Why don't you charge for your programs and retreats?

There are six activities for a brahmin, a knower of the supreme divinity: to learn, to teach, to worship for oneself, to worship for others, to give what you can and to accept what is offered in love and respect. A vaishya is a businessman and he charges for his services. A brahmin gives what he can and accepts what is offered. We try to live the life of brahmins. We work and accept what is offered with respect.

What's wrong with charging for a program?

If you knew God, would you want to turn that knowledge into an income stream? Wouldn't you have the faith that God will take care of you as you make your contribution to this world?

So charging would indicate a lack of faith in God?

It not only indicates a lack of faith, but your mind goes into the mechanics of how to make this business enterprise

successful. "How do I get more money?" Whereas, if all you want is to love God, then everything you need will come.

So you get into a certain frame of mind when it becomes a business.

As soon as you make it a business. Our definition of spirituality is giving more than you take. What we call business is getting more than you give. So the two are in opposition. As soon as you make spirituality your business, you can't stay in business, because you will want to give it all away. We have said, "We won't charge, and if people appreciate our contribution they will help us continue. If they don't, we won't continue. We'll go back to a mountain top and sit and chant the *Chandi*. That's fine. It doesn't hurt us in any way."

In business you need your clients, so you are dependent on them, and in spirituality you don't need anything. We don't need to share what we have. We are not trying to impose our ideology on anyone. So we are not trying to create an organization or build new buildings or finance a mortgage. We don't want any of that. That's why we don't charge.

How do you feel about debt?

We are seeking freedom. When you incur debt, what you are saying is, "I am going to enjoy today and pay tomorrow." So you are obligating yourself tomorrow for today's pleasure. Now, a businessman says, "That's probably a good idea, because tomorrow there will be inflation, and you can pay back today's pleasure at a lower rate than you would if you bought it for cash." We would say that's not a good idea from a spiritual point of view. If you encumber yourself for tomorrow, then you won't be free today. You have obligated yourself to spend your time working in the marketplace in order to pay for yesterday's enjoyment. You are borrowing karma.

Does debt affect our meditation?

Absolutely. You have to go to work to do what you don't want to do to pay off what you enjoyed yesterday.

216

But even if we didn't have debt, we'd still have to go to work to pay for lodging and food.

Not necessarily. You might create a different standard of life and spend less time working. Then you could work for God instead, and whatever you need will come to you.

So the debt ties you into a certain life-style for the future.

Yes. You can say, "I will buy a five thousand dollar car with cash instead of a fifteen thousand dollar car with credit. I will live within my means instead of trying to live more comfortably and obligating myself to do something in three to five years that I don't want to do when that time arrives."

20
A Story About Swami

Shortly after I met Shree Maa and Swami, there was a celebration at their temple for Mother's Day. At the end of the day, people came up to Shree Maa to receive a blessing. Swami was sitting next to her.

People greet Shree Maa in various ways. Some just say, "Hi," others offer a polite bow, and some touch their head all the way to the ground as a sign of ultimate respect, a common greeting for Gurus in India.

I had gotten in the habit of bowing to Shree Maa all the way down to the ground. This act of surrender usually filled me with deep peace.

Greeting Swami was an entirely different matter, however. At that point, Swami was someone whom I respected as a teacher, but he was — how else can I say it? — white. He was an American; he was like me, not an exotic saint from India. So I usually greeted him with a "Hi, Swami!"

On this day, however, many Indians were in attendance and they were giving Swami the big time bow, a full head to the floor number. It seemed like this event called for a special

greeting, yet it didn't feel right to give him the full Guru treatment. I decided on a compromise. I'd give him a half bow from the waist.

When I arrived in front of Swami, I smiled and gave him my half bow. He smiled broadly and bowed all the way to the ground in front of me.

I sat there, ego intact, seeing what a great lesson he taught me.

"WE ARE ALL GODS AND GODDESSES THINKING THAT WE ARE HUMAN BEINGS."

— Swami Satyananda

· BOOK THREE ·

CONVERSATIONS WITH SHREE MAA AND SWAMI SATYANANDA

Relationships

21

MEN AND WOMEN, WHAT'S THE POINT?

Why do you think so many marriages end in divorce in this country?

Shree Maa: This country? I think it's all over the world. Relationships have become competitive instead of being a place to learn respect. Everybody wants to win, but where is the peace?

So competition and selfishness are at the root of the problem?

Shree Maa: Yes. We haven't learned how to give. If each person would practice giving to their partner, their relationships would be peaceful and harmonious. Instead, most of us are very selfish. We are only thinking about ourselves. Therefore, in the Indian system, this time in the history of the planet is called the Dark Age.

Another reason for unsuccessful relationships is overpopulation.

How does overpopulation affect our relationships?

Shree Maa: People are increasing the population, but they don't have a goal or purpose. They are bringing souls to the earth and not teaching them spiritual wisdom.

What is the purpose of coming to the earth?

Shree Maa: Everybody has his or her own purpose. For example, you. You are a psychologist, but you did not know the real reason why you became a psychologist. You thought of counseling as just an occupation. You didn't look inside and find your real purpose, which was to give to this world. You were talking about relationships, but you didn't know the highest truth yourself. You took an intellectual approach, but you didn't go inside and realize that this was your way to give. Now you are understanding your real purpose for being a psychologist.

So it starts with knowing what your purpose is?

Shree Maa: Yes, but very few people have God's grace to truly understand their purpose in life. Swamiji and I were born with the grace to understand our purpose, even though the other people in our families were very different from us. It's a real problem if you don't understand your purpose.

Would you say that most people don't understand their purpose?

Shree Maa: Absolutely.

What does a person do who doesn't have a purpose?

Swami: I suggest that a person without a purpose better find one. Without a purpose it is difficult to have a meaningful life. How can you accomplish anything if you don't know what your goal is? We need to find a goal in life that would be worthy of our commitment.

Certainly our goal in life wouldn't be to have a transient relationship with someone who doesn't have a purpose either. That's where most of us make a mistake. We don't have a purpose of our own and we feel empty and look for another person to give us fulfillment. And they don't have a purpose either. Then we have two people without a purpose, trying to give each other's life meaning. We know the honeymoon period doesn't last. It's hard enough when you have a partnership with common goals. But if you don't have common goals, and the purpose of your relationship is just to assuage your loneliness, then as soon as your needs are no longer being fulfilled, the relationship is history.

The best thing to do is to stop and think, "What would be a commitment worthy of my dedication? What do I want to give to this world?"

What are some examples of a purpose?

Swami: Some people dedicate themselves to the environment, some to world peace, some to music, some to art, some to having a family and raising children.

Shree Maa: Everyone is different. The foremost objective is for them to give respect to their actions and show respect through their actions.

What do you mean by respect?

Swami: To have peace and joy and love in your heart; to love enough to give all your attention to the exclusion of the wandering mind and selfish desire.

If two people are performing their actions with that kind of respect, what does that look like? I don't think many of us have seen that kind of relationship.

Shree Maa: Whatever act they are performing gives birth to peace.

Swami: They treat each other with respect, and their communications are never harsh and always inviting. Other people like to be near them just because they show that kind of respect to each other. They nourish each other and those around them. They have a sense of security which energizes them, and that energy allows them to be competent and successful. They are able to enlist participation in their projects. Instead of struggling with life, they are able to flow with life. Because they have pure motivation, nature supports them in what they are trying to do. When nature supports them, the whole community wants to support them.

So most people are in relationships that are selfish.

Shree Maa: They're in relationships that are selfish because nowadays there are too many distractions. There are so many things we want to acquire. This grasping creates a lack of balance.

We have manipulated science for our selfish gain, and that is an indication of potential catastrophe. Only when wisdom and science are in harmony will we have peace.

I think many people know that selfishness is at the core of their relationship problems. I think they know they are selfish and they would have better relationships if they were able to give more, but they may not know how to change. Do you have any suggestions?

Shree Maa: If they will just begin to surrender their selfishness, their very first attempts will give them the answer to their question. That will give them the inspiration to strive with greater consistency.

If they feel good when they are giving, is that a sign that they are really giving?

Shree Maa: Yes. When they feel good, they will try to give more.

Swami: The first step in making a change is to do something for somebody else. That's a wonderful place to start. You could start by urging yourself to smile at the people you meet and say, "Good morning." Make a change in your life and surrender some selfishness, and see if you don't feel better.

What is the purpose of men and women having a relationship?

Shree Maa: For the illumination of true consciousness and bliss, it is necessary for the masculine and feminine principles to unite, for men and women to harmonize their various natures to work together.

Swami: When you put the qualities of men and women together, you have a more dynamic capacity for working effectively in creation. If a man can treat a woman like a Goddess, she will turn him into a God. If a woman can treat her man like a God, he will make her into a Goddess.

How do you treat someone like a God or a Goddess?

Shree Maa: Love and respect them with all your heart.

Swami: Completely surrender to your partner.

Shree Maa: This body is not eternal. Inside is God. You have to wake up!

You have to see the God within?

Shree Maa: Yes!

How do you do that?

Shree Maa: How did you get here?

You mean here to this ashram (laughing, not knowing where she is going)?

Shree Maa: Do you think you decided to come here, or did somebody send for you?

Somebody sent for me?

Shree Maa: Yes. The divine power.

Swami: Who told you to come to this ashram? The consciousness within you. The divine spark said, "I want to find out what those people are doing, to see if they have something I can add to my life." That was the divine being within you. If we can pay respect to that being within our partner, we can recognize their Godliness.

That's hard. We tend to see the personality and the body, and we don't see the God within the other person.

Shree Maa: Yes, nowadays it is very hard.

Swami: Having a relationship is a sadhana, a spiritual discipline.

Do you have any suggestions for how people can see God in their partners?

229

Swami: We suggest learning puja or worship, which trains you to see the God within.

So if you practice performing worship to a Goddess, you will be better able to see the Goddess in your partner?

Swami: Yes, and you can perform puja to your spouse, which will help you see the God within him or her.

Let's say you are with your partner, and she is doing something that irritates you, and you are upset with her. For instance, she left her dishes in the sink. How do you see the God in her at a moment like that?

Swami: In these kinds of situations, we want to develop the kind of communication where we can discuss any problems that arise. Those moments will occur, but they can be diffused with appropriate communication. If we have our goal in front of us, we can overlook the minor irritations. For example, Shree Maa sees me working on the computer for this *Chandi* project. In recognition of this, she is not demanding that I do the dishes. When I leave the dishes in the sink, she says, "The best interest of the ashram, the bigger goal, is to finish the *Chandi* project. So I will gladly wash his dishes." In a healthy relationship, we will find a way to talk about everything.

There is a beautiful verse in the *Lalita Trishati* that I am very fond of. It says, "Shiva and Shakti revolve around each other mutually and reciprocally. He who understands this understands what a chakra is." A chakra means a center of energy and it means a cyclical rotation. He who understands this reciprocity will surrender his ego and the egotism of minor irritations in order to be in harmony with the one divinity. If there is a persistent problem, it has to be communicated in an effective way. Otherwise, it will breed disharmony.

What you just said about communication is basically what a psychologist would say. I think that's very good advice, but I am trying to understand how you can see God in your partner when you are not liking their action in the moment. I find that very difficult.

Shree Maa: You have to prepare yourself internally first, so that you can see everything as God.

So you have to do a lot of sadhana and work on yourself. Then when you can see God everywhere, you can see God in your partner.

Shree Maa: Yes.

Is this the goal?

Shree Maa: The foremost objective in human life is to attain Godliness, which is liberation. Liberation is the cessation of all pain, all bonds and every type of deficiency. In order to obtain liberation, it is imperative to perform sadhana.

The purpose of all activity is to be liberated from all bonds and to find pure joy and true wealth. Whatever work you

231

perform, the ultimate objective is to attain Godliness. If you are aware of your ultimate objective while you are working, your mind, intellect and senses will be in harmony and your actions will move you toward liberation. This is what we call performing our dharma and finding our ideal of perfection.

What do you mean by ideal of perfection?

Swami: Every atom of existence has an ideal of perfection that it is striving to manifest. So the flower is trying to become the ideal flower. You are trying to manifest pure devotion.

Shree Maa: When you became a psychologist, you only wanted an occupation. You weren't thinking of the ideal of perfection. Now that you understand your ideal of perfection, you want to give, give to others.

Does that mean being perfect yourself?

Shree Maa: Even trying to be perfect is enough.

Is it possible to be perfect?

Shree Maa smiles radiantly and slowly nods her head, "Yes."

When you say "attain to Godliness," what does that mean?

Swami: Godliness is that state of perfection.

So it looks like it is going to be hard to explain this in words.

Shree Maa: Why?

Isn't it?

Shree Maa: I don't think so. When you have the right attitude, you will experience it directly.

Is that the purpose of relationships, to experience that state of perfection?

Swami: Sure. Relationships require us to surrender our selfishness, and in doing that we attain Godliness.

I know many people have trouble with the concept of surrender. I bet when they hear that they'll think, "I surrendered to Joe, and he cheated on me and broke my heart."

Shree Maa: We are talking about surrendering your ego. You have to surrender to your own self.

So you're talking about surrendering to the God within you.

Shree Maa: Yes. We are not talking about surrendering blindly.

Swami: When we talk about surrender, it does not absolve us from discriminating. In surrender, we offer ourselves in equilibrium to the God within our partner and ourselves. That doesn't mean we obey their every order. We have a duty to discriminate what is part of my path and what is not. Then we'll say to our partner, "Please explain to me how what you are asking is going to manifest our purpose, our highest Godliness. If it does, I'll probably be all for it. If it doesn't, I still respect the God within you, but I can't do what you want in this case."

Is it enough for one person to surrender, or do both need to surrender?

Shree Maa: If you live together, it is important that both people surrender.

What if you live with somebody who doesn't want to surrender?

Shree Maa: You will never find peace.

So you have to find somebody who has the same purpose.

Shree Maa: Yes. That is what we are trying to say. That is the only way you can find peace in your relationship, that is the way you can grow, that is the way you can inspire beautiful children in the way of dharma.

What do you do if your partner is sabotaging your spiritual practices? Let's say they make fun of your meditations, but you really love them and otherwise you get along?

Shree Maa: We are back to our first discussion. Why would we have a relationship without a common goal?

Swami: If you do have a relationship without a common goal, you had better stop right now and say, "Partner, what is the purpose of our being together, and how can we make that purpose manifest itself? If we can't manifest our purpose together, let's be honest about it and either make it happen alone or with another partner. Let's see how we can negotiate, how we can support each other's goals; otherwise, both of us will have to come back to this planet and start all over again."

So you are saying that our purpose is more important than anything else.

Swami: The romance, the attachment, the infatuation, the honeymoon period are so transitory. Unless we have a common goal, it will be very difficult to make it through life. As soon as we wake up and become aware of this, let's get to the business of defining our purpose and working together to make it manifest.

22

Your Mate, Your Fate And The Stars

Many spiritual seekers believe that it is better to walk the spiritual path alone. Is it more spiritually advanced to not be in a relationship when you are a serious seeker?

Shree Maa: God made this creation with both Shiva and Shakti. The greatest ideal is to illuminate divinity through the vehicle of relationships. Those who wish to perform sadhana and spiritual practices by themselves will not be able to be completely victorious over all aspects of their lives. There is a need to share, if not with one partner, then with the whole world.

Yes, but I'm curious where that leaves someone like me, since I'm not in a relationship and I don't think I want to be in one.

Shree Maa: You are done with relationships. We say when we become fifty years old, we finish with the householder ashram (stage of life) and we move toward sannyasa. At that time we go alone and we become detached from everything. Therefore, God made the four ashrams.

Is one usually around fifty when they feel they have completed the householder ashram?

Shree Maa: One rule of thumb is when you have lived approximately half of your life. But who knows how much longer you will be alive? Who knows?

How should we deal with the loneliness of not having a partner? Is there a lesson to be learned in that situation?

Swami: Yes, there is a lesson. The reason we don't have a partner is because *we* are not a good partner. We should cultivate a partnership with God. When we are alone but not lonely, we will become a good partner. If you are lonely and don't want to be alone, and you meet someone who is lonely and doesn't want to be alone, then you start a relationship based on fulfilling each other's needs. That's not the same as having a relationship because I love you and have something to contribute to you. Once you have a relationship with God and you have Her inside and you are not lonely, you have a direction in life. Then you can find someone with a similar direction with whom you can relate on many different levels at the same time.

Do you think that if a person has a good relationship with God, it would make finding a partner more likely?

Swami: Certainly.

Couldn't it be their karma to not be in a relationship?

Swami: Yes. But highly unlikely. If you have a relationship with God, you will automatically come to a point where you will have a relationship with God's children. You have to give your love away in order to make it grow.

But that relationship doesn't have to be with a romantic partner. It could be with a Guru, right?

Swami: Certainly. And then ultimately with your disciples.

Do you advise celibacy for someone who is single?

Shree Maa: It depends on the kind of person they are and what their nature is. Every individual will feel for themselves what is right for them.

Swami: My suggestion is promiscuity brings confusion and conflict, and relationships without commitment don't bring satisfaction. They create a transitory fulfillment on a very superficial level, and there remains an unfulfilled need to be accepted one hundred percent. Celibacy is a fact of life, not a discipline. Many people practice celibacy by thinking about what they are trying to avoid. We carry our desire with us and perceive the world through an unfulfilled desire. So real celibacy, I believe, is not a practice. It is where the thought doesn't come to our minds. As long as the thought comes to our mind and we are forcefully restraining ourselves, we are practicing celibacy, not living it.

Shree Maa: Ramakrishna told a story about a man who went to a prostitute, while his friend was listening to the *Bhagavad Gita*. The man who was enjoying with the prostitute was thinking, "My friend is thinking about God. I would like to do that, too." The man listening to the *Bhagavad Gita* was thinking, "I'm so pious, and my friend is such a bad person." The man who went to the prostitute and thought well of his friend and longed for God received positive karma, and the man who was thinking negatively about his friend received negative karma. It's all in the mind.

Isn't it a good idea to store and not dissipate energy?

Swami: It is when celibacy is a fact of life and not a practice of life. As long as you are thinking, "I shouldn't be thinking what I am thinking about," then you are not saving any energy by not fulfilling your desire.

Shree Maa: It's all in the mind.

Swami: Certainly there are practices where you bring the ojas up and you meditate on the flow of the subtle form of semen flowing up, and this is extremely energizing. There are many, many times when I got up from the fire ceremony after many hours and said, "This is much better than sex!"

Shree Maa: That's true.

Swami: There is an energy flow there, but if you sit in meditation and think, "I shouldn't be thinking about sex," it is a total waste of your energy not to have sex. It's counterproductive.

What is the best way to choose a partner?

Shree Maa: That's a good question.

Swami: The best way to begin to search for a partner is to clarify your goals. What do you want? What are your values? What is important to you? What is your life-style? From that understanding of what you want, you can ask potential partners what their goal in life is. You can develop a list of issues that are important to you. Then you have to determine if people are giving you the answers they think you want to hear, or if they are sincere.

Next, get involved in pursuing your goal. When you do that, you automatically come into contact with other people who have similar goals. You are liable to meet someone in the context of that pursuit, rather than finding someone who has no long-term goal or vision.

What is falling in love? That's the way most people in the West pick a partner. They fall in love and think, "I must be with the right person, because I'm having the 'falling in love' experience." But later they often realize they chose the wrong partner.

Swami: Most of the people I've observed in romantic love affairs seem to be escaping from their loneliness. They are missing something and they hope that it will be fulfilled by the person they're in love with. When they meet, they think, "Now I'm not alone. My deficiency is filled. I can't be such a bad person, because this person loves me." The acceptance from that special person gives birth to the feeling of falling in love.

So if you know what your purpose is and you are following it, you won't feel that lack and will be less likely to fall in love?

Swami: You still have the capacity to fall in love, but you won't fall in love with someone who isn't going in the same direction as you. You will find someone who uses similar tools and a similar language to express their love.

When two people are attracted to and feel familiar with each other, is a past life connection occurring?

Shree Maa: When we have an experience of a relationship from a past life, it is not necessarily a romantic attraction. It is not because a deficiency is being fulfilled. When we come together because of past life samskaras, it feels like a partnership between two people working towards a common goal.

What is the logic behind arranged marriages in India? That approach to choosing mates seems very strange to Westerners.

Shree Maa: First, someone looks at your horoscope. From looking at the horoscope, they determine what you should do on this earth, what are your basic tendencies and what are your strengths and weaknesses.

Are they accurate?

Shree Maa: If it is a good astrologer.

Would that be helpful for people in this country?

Shree Maa: Yes, but it is hard to find a good astrologer here. One has to do tapasya (spiritual practices) to be a good astrologer. These days it's a business, but in olden times, an astrologer would also be a sadhu. Every family has their own Guru, and the family Guru would create the charts. The Guru had no selfish interest.

My family follows their charts every year, and those charts are accurate. When the time for someone to get married arrives, they try to find the partner whose chart is appropriately harmonious for that person.

Is your fate in the stars? What does the chart tell you?

Shree Maa: We are born on this earth, but we have a relationship with the whole universe. Various planets at various times are closer to us and they have a greater capacity to attract our energies. When we take birth, an astrologer determines which planets are closest to us and which planets are most influential in our growth and development. Some of the planets have malevolent influences, which can be cured through our sadhana.

Those who don't have as much faith in God can cure those influences by wearing stones and amulets, but still you have to do some tapasya. For instance, you can wear a stone and fast on Tuesdays. You give up something for God.

In India we perform spiritual disciplines and, following the suggestions of our Guru, choose our partners and get married in harmony with the astrological charts. Generally we are at peace, because we get married in order to fulfill our dharma in a committed partnership, and there is an elder, respected individual of authority who is party to the relationship and who can mediate any potential conflicts and show us how to give up our selfish attachments.

Before coming into this lifetime, do we decide who we are going to have as a partner?

Shree Maa: I believe we do, but it looks like they don't believe that in this country. They think they choose their partners. But ultimately God does.

It's all planned in a way. Is that why the astrologers can read our charts?

Shree Maa: Our belief in the Indian culture is that birth, death and marriage are written before we come into this world.

I'm still not clear if we are choosing our partners or if God is choosing our partners?

Shree Maa: All relationships are created by previous karma.

Swami: All of us are children of a mother and a father. Lord Shiva is the Lord of Free Will. He says, "You can choose your partner." The Divine Mother is the Mother of the Fruit

243

of your Karma. She says, "As you sow, so you shall reap." We are all the children of both father and mother. We will get the fruit of our karma and we have the choice of whether or not we want to change it. Both are occurring at the same time.

Shree Maa: Ultimately we have to change, and that is God's blessing.

Swami: When we are confronted with a circumstance, we think we have a choice. Maybe we do and maybe we don't. But whatever we decide, we can do it with full attention, with an open heart and with the greatest degree of perfection.

When Shree Maa said that birth, death and marriage are already decided, are we talking about samskaras? Last lifetime there was a desire, and that created the current circumstances and that can be changed.

Swami: Yes.

Shree Maa: You are changing.

Swami: You are changing right now, and that's why you are asking these questions.

If we are choosing our partners, why would we chose to be in a painful marriage?

Shree Maa: Because you chose your partners with a selfish desire; therefore, it was painful. You didn't have a common goal.

So before we come into this body, we may choose a partner for this lifetime for the wrong reason?

Shree Maa: People do that and they suffer.

That's not very smart (laughing).

Shree Maa: But that is a samskara.

Swami: What you sow is what you will reap. If you don't reap it all in this lifetime, you'll get it in the next one. You will enjoy the fruit of your karma, whether you like it or not.

So we wanted it at some point.

Swami: We wanted it and we earned it. We deserved it.

If we had done lots of sadhana previously, why would we want that?

Swami: Because there was an unfulfilled desire for romantic relationships, and we went for the romance instead of for God.

So maya is so strong that even someone who has done a lot of sadhana would make that kind of choice?

Shree Maa: Yes, maya is very strong.

Swami: There is a story of Bharata, who was the king of India and was also a great sadhu and wise man. He went off into the forest and practiced the most severe austerities.

245

One day a pregnant deer came running through the ashram pursued by a lion. The lion jumped on the mother deer and killed her, and the mother gave birth to a baby deer just before she died. Bharata came out and scolded the lion, and the lion was afraid of Bharata and ran away.

Then the King took the baby deer and washed it and fed it and took care of it. When Bharata sat in meditation, the doe would sit with him and be very loving. Soon Bharata was always thinking about the deer. So when Bharata left his body, even though he was a great rishi, he was reborn as a deer. When he became a deer, he said to himself, "When I had a human birth, I wasted my time thinking about a deer. Now I will spend this lifetime thinking about God." When he left his body as a deer, he was reborn as a rishi. He never let any attachments sway him from his path. He said, "Look how subtle maya is. There I was on the precipice of realization, and I had to take a birth as a deer."

Is that why so many yogis come to this country and fall off the path?

Shree Maa: Not just this country. Everywhere.

Swami: But more so in this country, because of the promiscuity here. It is more natural for people in this country to fulfill the desires of the body.

Shree Maa: (Laughing) We are forgetting our own souls. We are entrapped by the five elements. Entrapped by the five elements, the supreme divinity lies down and cries.

So it's easier when you leave the human body and aren't trapped by the five elements?

Shree Maa: Yes! The body is a house. You live in the body with attachments and selfish desires. When we leave the body, we are free. Free (laughing)!

Swami: However, without this vehicle it is impossible to attain that state of liberation of which you speak. If you are not free when you are in the body, you cannot be free when you leave the body. It is not as if you are enlightened as soon as you die.

Shree Maa: No, you won't be enlightened, but you'll be free from the concerns of the body.

So the body is calling to us, saying, "Feed me. I'm hungry," and that's a trap. But when we let go of the body, our mind can still trap us?

Swami: If your mind was absorbed in wisdom when you were in the body, then when you leave the body, your mind will stay absorbed in wisdom. But if you have worldly attachments, when you are about to leave the body your mind will say, "I don't want to die. I don't want to go. Please, don't take me. I'm not ready to leave all my attachments!" How many people are saying at the time of death, "I'm not ready." We believe it's much more prudent to say, "Thanks for taking me."

If maya is so strong that someone like Bharata became attached, it seems like it's really hard to get to the top of the mountain.

Swami: Well, it's the only game in town.

Is that why you need a good Guru?

Shree Maa: Yes.

Swami: That's why we need to be good disciples.

"Mother, Mother, Mother!"

"Mother, Mother, Mother! Everyone foolishly assumes that his clock alone tells correct time. Christians claim to possess exclusive truth, and even modern liberal thinkers reiterate the same claim to exclusivity. Countless varieties of Hindus insist that their sect, no matter how small and insignificant, expresses the ultimate position. Devout Muslims maintain that Koranic revelation supersedes all others. The entire world is being driven insane by this single phrase: 'My religion alone is true.'

"O Mother, you have shown me that no clock is entirely accurate. Only the transcendent sun of knowledge remains on time. Who can make a system from Divine Mystery? But if any sincere practitioner, within whatever culture or religion, prays and meditates with great devotion and commitment to Truth alone, Your Grace will flood his mind and heart, O Mother. His particular sacred tradition will be opened and illuminated. He will reach the one goal of spiritual evolution.

"Mother, Mother, Mother! How I long to pray with sincere Christians in their churches and to bow and prostrate with devoted Muslims in their mosques! All religions are glorious! Yet if I display too much freedom, every religious community will become angry with me. I might even be forbidden to enter Your Temple again, O blissful Kali.

"Therefore take me secretly into the sanctuary of every tradition without exception, and I will worship ceaselessly with all humanity, night and day."

— *Ramakrishna, 19th century Indian saint*
From Great Swan, Meetings with Ramakrishna *by Lex Hixon*

251

The Human Melodrama

23

Ramakrishna

What was Ramakrishna's message?

Shree Maa: He showed us how to live simply, how to live with God in every moment. He didn't perform his sadhana in a remote jungle, but in a temple near Calcutta.

Swami: Ramakrishna embodied so many messages. His primary philosophy, put succinctly, was, "There are as many ways to proceed toward God as there are individuals." So you have a message of universality, a message in which every individual is responsible for defining his or her own dharma or ideal of perfection. To talk about the message of Ramakrishna is to define total acceptance of all of life. His message was also to experience total abandonment and love and joy in the process.

What was it like to be with Ramakrishna?

Swami: To be in his presence was to be holding the sides of your stomach all the time from laughing. It was to be filled with joy and excitement and enthusiasm and love and admiration.

There was always something going on. There was never a dull moment. Even in the silence, there was such a bhava (spiritual feeling), such an attitude and such a solemnity. When he would open his eyes, he would tell stories, and every story had a funny punch line. He was an irresistible storyteller who captivated his audience. He arrested their wandering minds. The center of all the culture of Calcutta was in this little room on the wing of the temple in Dakshineshwar. Everybody came to that little room to get nourished. It wasn't just information they received. They received his energy. They got the bhava of Ramakrishna.

He would sing in ecstasy. He would listen to other people sing. He would dance. He would jump up to look at the moon and run inside and call all his disciples who were asleep on the floor and yell, "Get up! Get up! You have to look at the moon right now!" They all got up and started to get dressed, and he said, "What are you doing? Who has time to think about clothes? Be a lover!" Then he ran outside stark naked and danced in the moonlight. I mean, we are talking about an ecstatic mystic!

Every moment in his presence was filled with this effervescent enjoyment and enthusiasm. There was always music, there was always dancing, there was always story-telling, there was always literature. Visitors came to see him, and there were blessings and songs and stories. Intellectuals would come and debate philosophies, and the disciples would snicker in the background, "Oh, here comes another one who thinks he knows so much. He thinks he's going to defeat our Guru in debate." So there was this mixture of activities going on day and night. He slept very little, and the party went on continuously.

Shree Maa: There was bhava all the time.

Swami: All the time. And his wife, Sharada Maa, fed everyone. She was a fountain of wisdom and a fountain of grace. She was so surrendered to Ramakrishna and worshiped him so purely that she became him.

Shree Maa: He demonstrated how to live with pure love all the time. He didn't just demonstrate how to perform sadhana. He showed human beings how to live simply, with pure love.

Swami: His examples were pulled out of the lives of normal people. He was so observant. He would talk to the village people in their own language. He would use analogies from the kitchen in order to describe states of consciousness. He would talk to the farmers and use analogies from the farm.

Shree Maa: He used a servant as one example. She was working in somebody else's house, but all the time she was thinking about the people of her village. Ramakrishna said, "We should be like that. We come into this world temporarily. While we are in this temporary house, we should always remember our real home."

When he was with children, he would play their games with them. When he was with young boys, he would joke with

255

them and use slang language. When he was with adults, he would talk like an adult.

Swami: He was a perfect chameleon. He would blend with whoever was with him.

He would give to each person what they needed.

Swami: Right. He would immediately find the common language with people. Whether they were village people or sophisticated people, educated or uneducated, children or adults, he would find the appropriate language to describe the most beautiful states of consciousness.

Shree Maa: He was always joyful, always loving. Once he was joking with a few young boys and then suddenly he became silent. He looked at Hanuman's picture for a long time and then he said, "Look at the bhava of Hanuman. Look at what he stands for. He doesn't care about wealth. He doesn't care about the comfort of his body. He only wants God.

"When Hanuman was fleeing Lanka with the brahmastra (divine weapon), Mandodari, Ravana's wife, tried to entice him with many fruits. She said, 'Hey, monkey, eat this fruit and leave that weapon here.' She thought the monkey, in his desire for these fruits, would leave the brahmastra that he stole from Ravana. But Hanuman was not a foolish child. He said, 'You think I have any lack of fruit! The fruit that I have found is the fruit of many births. The tree that gives the fruit of enlightenment is in the heart of Rama. Rama has taken form as the granter of all boons. Whatever fruit you will desire, that fruit you will receive. You speak of many fruits, but you leave the fruit that is best. Go to Rama and you will get every fruit.'"

Ramakrishna told this story and then he started crying and went into bhava samadhi. You can see how he captured everybody's mind.

Would he then get stiff and freeze into a pose like you see in one of his pictures?

Swami: Ramakrishna would enter into all kinds of samadhi. In this story he entered into bhava samadhi in which he would continue talking. His mind was totally absorbed in the deity about whom he was speaking. When he was in savikalpa samadhi, there was nothing but him and Maa. Then he would go into nirvikalpa samadhi, where he was Maa.

Shree Maa: It was pure love.

Ramakrishna was well-known in Calcutta, which was just eight kilometers from Dakshineshwar (where Ramakrishna lived), yet at any given time there was only a small group around him. Why weren't thousands of people mobbing his temple?

Swami: No great saint ever tried to attract a crowd. Ramakrishna wanted a few appropriate people. He tried to keep his presence hidden. He didn't want thousands of people coming to worship him. He wanted a few noble souls who would make a difference in this world.

Ramakrishna's nephew, Hriday, told him, "You should show your siddhis (spiritual powers). Pray to Mother for siddhis." Ramakrishna said, "What would I do with siddhis?" Hriday replied, "Many people will come, and you'll get lots of money and with that money you can build schools and hospitals." So Ramakrishna went to Kali and said, "Maa, Hriday says I should ask You for siddhis, so I can be rich and famous and powerful." Then he went into a swoon and lay on the floor and went into a very deep state of consciousness and reported a vision in which he saw an old lady covered with dung. The lady said to him, "When I was young and beautiful, you weren't interested in me. Now that I am old and covered with filth, do you have any more interest in me? That's what will happen if you get siddhis and become rich and famous. It's like covering a jewel with dirt." So Ramakrishna refused to touch money all through his life. He refused to ask for things of the world.

Keshab Sen also approached Ramakrishna and asked him why he didn't pray for more schools and hospitals so he could help the poor. Ramakrishna thought, "What a waste of my time. This is my opportunity to spend my time with the Divine Mother. It's not my job to maintain real estate."

I don't understand why he didn't want to build schools and hospitals.

Swami: He felt it was a worldly occupation of consciousness. Why would he want to focus on manifested existence?

But to serve people is to serve God. Isn't that what we are doing on this planet?

Swami: That's one of the things we're doing here. But some of us are so absorbed in God that they serve humanity by showing what it's like to be absorbed in God. His greater service was to be an example, because that is rarer and more needed than more hospitals.

Shree Maa: Oh, Shiva, Shiva. (Shree Maa lies down on her cot.)

Are you tired, Shree Maa?

Shree Maa: No, I'm in bhava (samadhi).

Swami: That's not fair. This is an interview (laughing). You're not allowed to go into samadhi during an interview.

24

THE COSMIC PLAY

What is a lila?

Shree Maa: You are doing a lila with us right now. Everything is lila. As long as we are living in this world, it is lila. It's playing a game. It's a drama.

Swami: Every action is a drama on the stage of consciousness. That is a lila. So by definition, nature, when manifest, will act. It is all part of the drama. If we see it as a drama in the play of God, then we side with Shakespeare and say the world is a stage.

Is that where the joy comes from?

Swami: That's the joy, because we lose our attachment to how things turn out. We become the witness. We become the audience of the lila of God. If we say, "I am the star of this play," then we feel pleasure and pain, because we want our play to be a certain way. We forget the author is somewhere else. It's not always going to be the way we want it to be.

It's not?

Swami: Otherwise, we would always remain in the bhava.

What is maya?

Swami: Maya is the definition of consciousness. Maya is the form of consciousness, the great exposer of consciousness, because she creates limitations by form.

I'm losing you.

Swami: Every object is a limitation of consciousness. The perception of every object is a perception of a limitation of consciousness, because if there were no objects, consciousness would perceive without limitation.

You have limited it. Put a finite form on it.

Swami: Yes. Maya is a limitation of consciousness. Lila is the action and interaction between the various limitations.

I have a question about Ramakrishna and lila. There is a story about one of Ramakrishna's devotees who had to go home by crossing the Ganges by boat. While he was crossing the river, a great storm arose. Ramakrishna was very worried and sent his disciples running out to discover if the devotee arrived home safely. Now, I would assume Ramakrishna has the ability to know whatever he wants to know. I assume he could tell if the devotee arrived safely without sending his devotees. Why was he so worried? Was that Ramakrishna's lila?

Shree Maa: Yes, it's a lila because he sent his devotees off so he could have a respite from them.

So he knew what happened to the devotee?

Shree Maa: Of course he knew!

Is all of life like that?

Swami: Absolutely. It's like Shree Maa telling me to go off this week and record the *Chandi*. She knows I am going to have to do it five times to get it right. She knows I haven't been chanting the *Chandi* lately, because I've been so involved in making a video.

Is that right, Shree Maa?

She nods, "Yes."

Swami: I know her lila.

But she didn't tell you that's why she was asking you to record the Chandi *at that particular time?*

Swami: No. She told me, "You must record the *Chandi* this week! It has to be done this week! You have to chant it everyday." I know her tricks. Otherwise, I'd be working on videos or writing another book. Maa is tricky.

(Swami lies down.)

Now you're lying down, too (laughing). I'm going to get a complex here.

Swami: Come join us. Find a space.

So, Shree Maa, if you ask someone to do something for you, like get you a glass of water, is there a purpose behind that request, beyond the obvious reason of needing water?

Shree Maa: I wouldn't ask that from just anybody.

But if you asked somebody to do something, is there a reason behind it?

Shree Maa: Yes.

I remember on the last U.S. tour when you were sick, many people were giving you medical advice and remedies. You allowed everyone to help you.

Swami: Yes, because everyone needed the opportunity to get involved in Shree Maa's personal life.

So it's a misunderstanding to take the drama too seriously. Is that why your teachings and Ramakrishna's teachings are so joyful?

Shree Maa: Yes.

But most people are taking their dramas very seriously.

Swami: Spirituality is a very serious business (laughing).

So many of us live our lives filled with tension and stress and pain, and the funny thing is, we are still so attached to our

life-styles. It's strange that so few of us see the lila in all of this.

Shree Maa: Because you are living with selfish desire. Even those doing spiritual practice do it from a place of "I, I, I." When we love God, we have to give. If we don't act unselfishly, we become serious. Ramakrishna taught, "I am the child of the Divine Mother." He did not feel that he was the one giving. He felt that the Mother was giving through him. Nowadays people don't feel that if they love God, God will do everything for them. There is so little trust and faith.

Swami: Because of that, we make a distinction between our spiritual practice and our material life. People think that they would love to quit their job so they can be spiritual. It is a faulty notion that spirituality is something separate from life. They believe that there is a worldly self and a spiritual self. That's not true. There is just the Self.

People think that the time to be spiritual is when they are meditating or performing a spiritual practice, but all the time is the time to be spiritual. Your spirituality cannot be awakened if you only do it a few moments a day or a few hours a day. It can only be awakened if you live a spiritual life. It cannot be awakened as a practice. It's not about practices. It's about being in love with life. Practices are valid because they remind us to live the spiritual life.

· BOOK FOUR ·
PUTTING IT ALL INTO PRACTICE

25
How to Choose A Practice

Swami, when Westerners look for a spiritual path, they find so many options: Buddhism, Hinduism, Sufism, and so on. How does one choose a spiritual path for oneself?

The only way to choose a path is through inspiration. We need to find the example, the Guru, who inspires us to choose that path. If we get inspired by a Buddhist or a Christian or a Muslim or a Hindu or a Jew, it doesn't make a bit of difference. We will find that the eternal ideal of perfection is attainable through any discipline that we pursue.

Lots of Westerners go from one path to another, from one inspiration to another, but don't stick to any path. What do you think of that?

That wasn't their true inspiration; it was a passing inspiration. There are many levels of inspiration. Some inspirations are so great they evoke commitment, and some are so transitory they inspire little or no commitment.

Is it possible to be inspired by something that is not your path, but just happens to be what is in front of you?

Sure.

Is that okay?

Certainly that's okay, and we will pursue it until we find that it's not our path and then we'll be ready for the next inspiration.

It will lead you to the next step.

Yes. We will search many paths until we find something that inspires us enough to make a commitment. Once we make a commitment, we can begin to practice.

Is that the inspiration we are looking for, something that is so satisfying that it will draw us toward practice?

Yes. And in the meantime, we follow every inspiration we get. We may get the inspiration to do the wrong thing for us, but eventually we'll realize that and leave that inspiration, because it no longer calls to us. We may get the inspiration to do the right thing for us and start it with a minimum of engagement and effort until we find that it's really neat. It will make us want to give more effort; it will pull us in.

It's not something you force yourself to do.

No. You don't meet someone and say, "I am going to force myself to fall in love with him or her." It just doesn't happen that way. You fall in love gradually or you fall in love head over heels at first sight. Either way, once we have made the commitment, we want to honor that commitment and pursue it with conviction.

We have so many distractions, so many demands on our time. We are so busy. It's difficult to follow a path with the kind of commitment you are talking about.

When you love so much that you don't think about all the distractions and you only think about your beloved, then you really are a lover.

Yes, but what do we need to do to get to that place?

You keep trying. You don't say, "Just because I didn't automatically fall in love at first sight, I'm not going to try it anymore." You take the small inspiration you do get and cultivate it. Try to put yourself in the position of a lover instead of waiting to be loved. First you become the lover, and after a while you become the beloved.

What do you mean by that?

I mean when you become a lover, you become the person you love the most. You know what it is like to love. So you give yourself over to that love. That is pure love without selfishness. You love yourself because you know your true self. When you know your true self, you know God. You know your beloved. You make friends with your best friend, the closest person to you, yourself. Then you cultivate that relationship. We can't expect love to just descend on poor, little, unworthy me. When we love God in such a way that we become a lover, then we are putting out the energy of love, and automatically it will come back to us.

You may choose the path of hatha yoga or sitting or chanting or study or whatever "ism" you choose. There are only a certain, limited number of practices. The mantras are different, the language is different, the customs are different. There's a little bit of a twist on the philosophy. But either you are going to sit down or stand up, sing or be quiet. Either you are going to focus inside or focus on one point outside. The practice is essentially the same. There are very few distinctions in the practice when you look at what people are doing.

What would you say is the common denominator in all those different practices?

One common denominator is the cultivation of satsangha, the association with people who are doing similar practices. In every "ism," in every path, in every religion, we have a congregation and we get together and do a number of different activities. We listen to the scriptures, which are the experiences of other people who have preceded us. We sit silently, we share music and we share food. We share good company. Satsangha is a bonding process, so that people within the congregation try to network their skills and talents and opportunities.

How important is that?

Very important. Satsangha creates an opportunity for people to grow by receiving inspiration and feedback from others who are practicing in a similar way.

Does it make the path more difficult if a person is a lone practitioner, living someplace where satsangha is hard to find?

Certainly. You want to maintain satsangha. We were just in Montana and we met a group of people who practice Sufi dancing. They created the Greater Rocky Mountain Sufi Dancing Club, and they dance together once a month. People come from Colorado, Montana, Idaho and North Dakota to dance. They drive three or four hundred miles, because they need to dance together. It is not enough to be off by yourself dancing. There comes a point in the evolution of every seeker where you want to dance together. We have to give it away in order to make it grow.

What about the sadhus in India who live in the mountains by themselves? Is that a different stage?

It is a different stage, but no one every stays on top of the mountain. They go up there, but no one stays. Either you don't find what you are looking for and you have to come down because you need a new inspiration, or the calls of the body require attention, or you do find what you are looking for and you have to come down to share it. In either case, you require satsangha. Nobody stays on top. You can climb to the top of the highest mountain and stay there for the longest period of time, like many yogis have, but every one of them came down.

26
GETTING STARTED

Where is a good place to start if you would like to experience the methods that you and Shree Maa teach?

You can start by repeating a mantra.

What is a mantra?

Mantra comes from the Sanskrit word "mantrayate," that which takes away the mind. When you focus on the mantra, you exclude all other thoughts, and in that way the mantra has taken away your mind. It has taken all the other thoughts away. To use the mantra to its optimum efficiency, we focus on it and get into the vibration and attitude of it, the bhava.

Every object of existence has two sets of names. One is a name that we have agreed to call it, a given name in whatever language it may be. It is the intellectual meaning. The other is its natural name. Within every object there is movement, there is vibration. There are protons, neutrons, electrons, quarks, all kinds of atomic and subatomic vibrations moving in a vortex of empty space. Every vibration produces a sound, whether audible to the ear or not, and every sound is expressible by a letter or word. These words and sounds are called the natural name of an object or feeling, known as the bija mantra, the abbreviated form of the subtle vibration, actually what the object is saying itself. That's its natural name.

The mantras, the words of Sanskrit, contain both the expressions of the natural names and the given names. The Sanskrit mantras denote a specific object or relationship or feeling, and they connote a special bhava or attitude and vibration, the feeling.

What happens when you repeat a mantra?

A mantra has a particular frequency. When you concentrate and repeat the mantra, you vibrate at the frequency of that mantra. You become one with the vibration of the mantra and resonate with its meaning.

What makes the vibration of the mantra so valuable?

A mantra is always a divine vibration. Mantras are words of power that take us to divinity.

So saying the mantra will take us to a divine state?

Saying the mantra or thinking the mantra or breathing the mantra fills our entire being with the mantra. The mantra becomes us. We become one with what the mantra stands for. We become one with God.

If you kept repeating the English word "love," for instance, would you get more of an intellectual understanding, but it wouldn't convey the same feeling the Sanskrit word for love would convey?

That's right. Although it might have a similar meaning, it doesn't have the same vibration. Also the Sanskrit word is more specific. In English, through a process of acculturation, we have assumed so many associations with the word love. We say, "I love your shirt," or "I love my girlfriend," or "I love God." We are using the same word to describe everything from the most superficial and transitory to the most idealistic and permanent kinds of love. When you say "love," I don't know exactly what you mean. However, the Sanskrit word "bhakti" means devotion to God, a very specific form of love. In addition, the word "bhakti" evokes the feeling it is talking about. If you say the mantra "bhakti" over and over again, you will get more into the feeling of devotion and love for God than by saying "love, love, love."

Should one choose a mantra by deciding what feeling one wants to evoke?

You could, or you could allow a Guru to choose mantras that would be more efficient in guiding you to the types of energies that you, as an individual, will want to inculcate.

So having a Guru might be the best way to get a mantra. What if you don't have a guru?

You could start with the mantra "Om Namah Shivaya" (pronounced "Om Namah Shivaaya"), which means "I bow to the Consciousness of Infinite Goodness."

Why that mantra?

Because Shiva is the Guru of all Gurus, and the five-lettered mantra is the most basic building block of all Sanskrit sadhana. From the five-lettered mantra, we go to the nine-lettered mantra, to the mantra with eleven syllables, and so on. It grows and grows in complexity, in sophistication and in the various qualities that a seeker will want to increase as he or she proceeds along the path. Start with the five-lettered mantra if you don't have a Guru. If you worship Shiva, He will send the Guru who is appropriate for your personal development.

When you worship any of the deities, you are worshiping all the other deities. Krishna in the *Bhagavad Gita* says, "Anyone who worships any other God is really worshiping Me." Now if you wanted to say Krishna's mantra, "Hare Krishna, Hare Krishna, Krishna Krishna, Hare Hare," that's one way of worshiping Shiva. If you want to say, "Shri Rama, Jaya Rama, Jaya Jaya Rama," that's fine too. Pick any one of the mantras that you know and use it. If you don't know a mantra, then say it in English.

Shiva

Let's say you choose to work with a mantra, for example, "Om Namah Shivaya." How do you work with that mantra?

You can create a ritual of worship, which will focus your mind and make it habituated to sitting still. We call that ritual of worship puja.

Puja is a guided meditation. It will calm your mind. All you have to do is follow the instructions and recite the mantras and you will be guided into a state of meditation. There are many forms of puja. A simple puja would begin by lighting a candle and a stick of incense and putting a flower on an altar. Then sit there for a few minutes and say, "Om Namah Shivaya," either internally or out loud. You can say it out loud at the beginning until it feels natural to recite it internally. You can keep your eyes closed or keep them open and look at your candle or your flower. From that simple puja, you can get more sophisticated and elaborate.

What do you do with your thoughts while you are repeating the mantra?

You try to let them go. Try not to pay attention to them. Every time you find yourself drifting into reverie, just bring yourself back very gradually and slowly and lightly, without forcing yourself, and say, "Om Namah Shivaya."

How long do you do that?

For as long as you choose. It is your relationship with God.

Are you supposed to sit in any particular way?

You can sit any way you like, but if you keep your backbone straight and your head erect, you will experience a greater state of alertness. It's helpful to sit in a state of attention.

Why is that important?

When you are slouching, it is impossible to draw a full breath; you only breathe very short breaths between the nose and the lungs. When your back is straight, you have the entire abdomen through which you can breathe. A state of attention helps us to breathe more deeply. So when we sit in a state of attention we can go inside and see that the deity to whom we are offering worship is inside us.

Can you say more about how we can see a deity like Shiva inside us?

Conceive of the greatest goodness that you possibly can conceive and then make it greater.

Do you visualize a picture of goodness?

A picture of goodness or a feeling of goodness. You could put that picture or feeling in your heart, or you could put it in your third eye. Just put goodness there and make it better and better until your chest expands and you feel that goodness exuding into the universe.

Is it helpful to have a little table to sit in front of where you can keep a candle?

Certainly. You don't want to put the candle on the carpet.

Or under the curtains.

Not recommended.

What do you put on the altar?

You can put anything that symbolizes divinity to you.

You just described a simple puja. What would one do if they wanted to try a more complicated puja?

We would recommend starting with either the beginner's Shiva puja or the beginner's Durga puja, which we have translated into English.

I want to add my testimonial to this discussion. Before I met you, I had been meditating for twenty-five years using various Buddhist and Hindu methods. I often became discouraged to find my mind still filled with thoughts during meditation. When I started performing pujas, I was surprised how easy it was. I just followed the directions and recited the mantras, and when the puja was finished my mind was usually quiet. It was great!

That's what they are designed to do.

Where do these particular pujas come from?

These pujas are several thousand years old. They were designed by rishis as a system of worship, as meditations to take their consciousness into the presence of divinity.

The rishis practiced these very same pujas?

Absolutely.

Is it significant that millions of people have practiced these pujas and recited these mantras? Does something carry over to us?

Yes. It has a whole lineage, a whole history and culture behind it. We are not making up things that come to our minds and passing them on as new truths that we discovered. We are taking an established tradition that came through a lineage of teachers and cultivating it. We are making it the base of our practice, from which we can append any of the other practices that are pertinent to our particular search.

So we could take the beginner's Shiva puja, for instance, and add a Christian prayer? Essentially, customize?

Absolutely. Pujas are designed as building blocks. They are modular, so that you can construct your own puja. Every individual will make his or her own puja. A puja is designed in such a way that once you have the basic structure and foundation in place, you can erect any kind of edifice that you choose upon that foundation.

Is there an attitude that is preferable while you perform a puja?

The attitude of gratitude. The appreciation of the privilege of getting to spend a few moments sitting with God.

So you are sitting with God?

Certainly. You are sitting with that consciousness of infinite goodness.

Do you need a teacher to practice these pujas?

The preliminary pujas that we are speaking of can be performed without the presence of a physical teacher. As we get more sophisticated in our forms of worship, we will want to consult more sophisticated teachers so we have an example of how the puja is performed and how the mantras are pronounced. They will give us instructions and indicate how we can enhance our puja.

Are you and Shree Maa available as teachers for people who are interested in learning pujas?

At times we are available for very dedicated students.

If someone wanted to get involved in more complicated pujas, can they get them from you?

Yes, we have the beginner's Shiva and Durga pujas, each of which takes about a half-an-hour to perform. We also have more sophisticated pujas that take three or more hours to perform.

How does performing a puja relate to leading a spiritual life?

Spiritual practices are valuable, because they remind us to live a spiritual life.

27
SHIVA AND DURGA PUJAS

If someone wants to practice a puja, where can they start?

We recommend the beginner's Shiva or Durga pujas. Both are easy to practice and take only about a half-an-hour to perform. They are guided meditations that you can follow step by step and that are designed to take you into a state of meditation.

Shiva Puja

The Shiva puja is a beautiful place to start. The Shiva mantra is the easiest, because it has only five letters: Na – Ma – Shi – Va – Ya. By worshiping Shiva, we cultivate the qualities of infinite consciousness, detachment and freedom from bondage to the material world.

Shiva is the Lord who causes transformation. He makes changes happen. Before we can construct a new edifice, we must excavate and clear the land. Shiva is the Lord of

Excavation. He makes changes happen by clearing the old and making way for the new.

Shiva takes away all fear. The transitory nature of existence makes us feel insecure. We want things to stay the way they are. Until we accept the will of Shiva, there will be fear. As long as we identify with the changes that are occurring, we create our own pain by our attachment to the way we think things should be.

Through Shiva we cultivate the attitude of perceiving intrinsic reality, not extrinsic appearance. We identify with that which does not change. We become the witnesses to the changes of nature. Remembering the eternal reality, we free ourselves from pain and fear. We see them as passing states of mind and accept the will of God.

Shiva is also the strength of willpower to define and obtain our goals. Nothing deflects Shiva from his path. Shiva gives us the strength to attach ourselves to the sustaining values of life, to the values that will stay with us through eternity.

Shiva is especially good for women and, in particular, married women. If they can see Shiva in a stone or a picture, they can more easily find Shiva in their spouse. With their loving devotion, they can make their spouse become more like Shiva.

When women worship Lord Shiva, they become more self-sufficient, stronger, clearer, more defined in their goals, much more resourceful and less dependent.

Shiva

Why would a man want to worship Shiva?

A man worshipping Shiva would take on the qualities of
Shiva. He would become a yogi. He would become
independent and would decrease the desires and the
needs of the body. He would increase his strength,
endurance, patience and sadhana.

*Is there a visualization or an image that one can associate
with Shiva when you are praying to him?*

You could envision the picture of Shiva in human form or you can picture the Shiva lingam or you can picture a flower or a candle or a picture of Shree Maa. You can envision Shiva living in every object in existence.

Would you also recommend meditating on the mantra "Om Namah Shivaya" after completing the puja?

Yes, I would. I would also recommend doing japa of that mantra when you first get up in the morning.

What is japa?

Japa is the continuous recitation of a mantra. You may want to set yourself a goal of ten malas (a mala is a string of 108 beads used for japa) or twenty malas or a hundred malas a day. Shree Maa is up by 3:00 AM, and I am up by 3:15 AM, and we usually do our japa and our meditation until 4 AM or 4:30 AM, and then we begin our pujas.

Would you suggest saying the mantra throughout the day?

I would suggest using the mantra as much as you can, in as many appropriate circumstances as possible. When you are washing dishes, when you are cleaning the house, when you are waiting in line or when you're about to go to sleep. There are so many functions that we all perform where we can keep the mantra going. There will come a time when you will hear the mantra going on inside, as though there is a tape recorder in the background. You won't have to pay attention to it, and it will be going all the time.

Durga Puja

Why would you suggest working with the beginner's Durga puja?

The qualities of the Divine Mother are compassion, service, gentility and sensitivity. By worshiping Durga, we inculcate the qualities of the Divine Mother; we make them our own. We emulate our Guru, our object of worship. So when men worship Durga, they become more sensitive, appreciative, and more capable of extending compassion and service to mankind.

Durga

All men who are attracted to or want to learn how to love
the Divine Mother can worship Durga. As they cultivate the
love of the Divine Mother, they can become the husband

291

and the devotee of the Divine Mother. They can also more easily see the Divine Mother in their spouse. The worship of Durga will make them Shiva.

How could worshiping Durga help a woman?

A woman worshiping the Divine Mother would become much more motherly, serviceful, sensitive and appreciative. She would become more creative and dynamic, with more power and energy. She would also become more fearless and courageous.

She would clarify her goals more distinctly so that she could become the energy of inspiration which takes her family to God. There's a Sanskrit quotation that says, "Give me a wife who is in harmony with my mind and can lead my family across this difficult ocean of worldliness."

Why did you choose Durga as the introductory Divine Mother puja?

"Durgam" means confusion, and Durga takes away the durgam. She is a form of the Mother that is sorely needed by spiritual seekers who are confronted with the complexities of life. We meet obstacles in reconciling our spiritual life with our material needs, and this creates confusion and a barrier that precludes us from attaining the goal. Durga is the Goddess who removes and eradicates all the barriers, obstacles, difficulties and self-imposed limitations that keep us from reconciling our spiritual and material lives.

It would be wonderful for couples to worship each other as Shiva and Durga.

What is the Durga mantra?

"Om Hrim Shrim Dum Durgayai Namah" (pronounced "Om Hreem Shreem Dum Durgaayai Namah"). The translation of this mantra is "Om. We bow to the Goddess Durga, the Grantor of Increase, who removes all difficulties."

So if you worship Shiva or Durga, you begin to develop their characteristics within yourself. That sounds similar to your earlier statements that loving and serving your Guru makes you become more like them.

There is a law of mutual conductivity that says when two of anything enter into a relationship, the dominant qualities will always be assumed by the other. So when the wind hits water, the wind becomes cool and the water makes ripples. When electricity touches the wire, the electricity follows the direction of the wire and the wire gets hot. When a disciple comes into a relationship with the Guru, the disciple begins to practice puja and the Guru accepts the disciple's karma.

The disciple refines his or her own self to become more and more like the Guru. The Guru tries to remain free from attachment, so when he takes the karma of the disciple, the Guru doesn't become bound by that karma. He takes away the attachment from the disciple, but doesn't cultivate attachment. Gurus are in a position to take the karma,

293

because they have freed themselves from attachment or they can recycle that karma very quickly.

Does the Guru actually take the karma away so the disciple doesn't have to experience it?

The disciples have to experience the fruit of their karma, but with the guidance and love of the Guru, that experience can be auspicious and beneficial. With the Guru's help, the disciples move very quickly beyond their karma, whereas, without the guidance of the Guru, the disciples take on the full karma and may dwell in it. They may sit there like a frog in a well.

If a disciple has negative karma, he experiences something, but it may not feel all that negative?

Or it may feel negative, but he moves beyond that negativity and completes that karma and makes changes in his life.

What a deal!

It's quite a deal. So that's why we say a Guru is someone who can assist us in performing our karma without becoming stuck in our karma himself.

Would all this occur if your Guru were Shiva or Durga?

Absolutely.

So by doing puja to Shiva or Durga, you are developing a relationship with them and with God and Guru. As a result, you take on their positive, divine qualities, and they take your negative karma.

Absolutely.

Wow!

Shiva is the Guru of all the Gurus. If you don't have a Guru and you accept Shiva as your Guru, ultimately Shiva is going to prepare you to receive a physical Guru. Then he'll send you the physical Guru when you are ready.

The deal keeps getting better!

Yes. So you can worship Shiva and then worship Durga, in other words, perform the beginner's Durga and Shiva pujas back to back or separately at different times of the day. Ultimately, we want to worship everyone. We want to worship all of life. That is what we are calling enlightenment, when all burdens have been removed, when nothing is heavy to us, and we are so light that we worship everything.

OM

PURNAM ADAH PURNAM IDAM

PURNAT PURNAM UDUCYATE,

PURNASYA PURNAM ADAYA

PURNAM EVAVASHISHYATE.

OM

That is whole and perfect, this is whole and perfect. From the whole and perfect, the whole and perfect becomes manifest. If the whole and perfect issue forth from the whole and perfect, still only the whole and perfect will remain.

297

OTHER PUBLICATIONS

If you would like to order any of the following books or CD's, please contact us at http://www.ShreeMaa.org

If you are interested in practicing puja:
Beginners' Shiva Puja
Beginners' Durga Puja
Advanced Shiva Puja and Yajna
Ganesh Puja
Hanuman Puja
Kali Puja

If you are interested in learning more about Shree Maa:
Shree Maa: The Life of a Saint, Biography of Shree Maa

If you are interested in learning more about Swami Satyananda:

Sahib Sadhu, The White Sadhu: Stories of Swami in India, Told By A Disciple

If you are interested in Shree Maa's music:
The Songs of Ramprasad
The Goddess is Everywhere
Shiva is in My Heart

298

If you are interested in listening to mantras on CD:
Lalita Trisati
The Thousand Names of Kali
Navarna Mantra

If you are interested in reading classical Sanskrit scripture:
Chandi Path
Bhagavad Gita
Devi Gita
Sundara Kanda
Guru Gita

**If you are interested in stories of Gods, Goddesses
and Sadhus:**
Swami Purana
Sadhu Stories from the Himalayas

Acknowledgments

Special thanks to the following people whose love, talent and generosity made this book possible:

Mary Keil

Radha Gaines

Virginia Hall